COWBOYS STADIUM

ARCHITECTURE · ART · ENTERTAINMENT
IN THE TWENTY-FIRST CENTURY

Rizzoli
NEW YORK

New York · Paris · London · Milan

TABLE OF CONTENTS

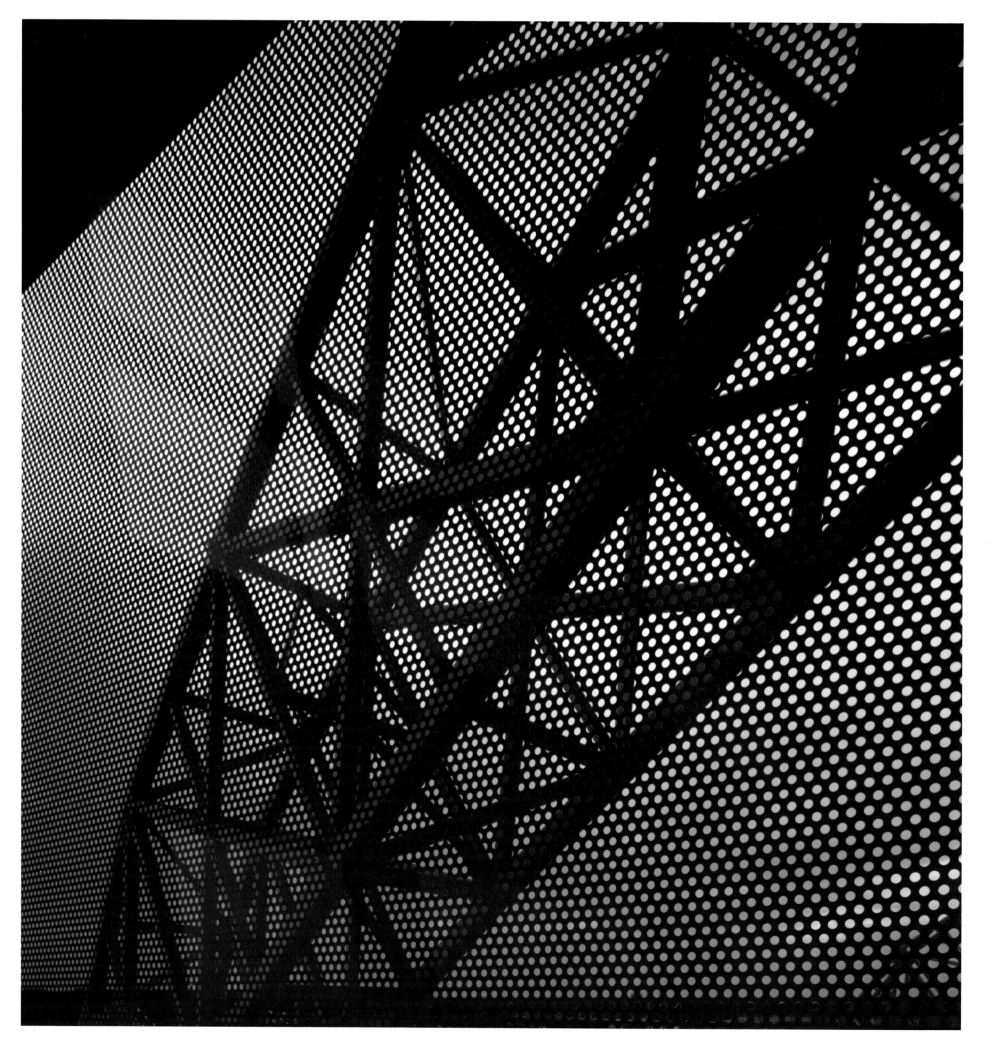

FOREWORD

BIG BEAUTY

The game of football is no different than the business of sports and sports entertainment. They all involve taking risks and thinking big. Throughout our years with the Cowboys we have embraced big risk taking and aggressive thinking. Those basic philosophies provided the inspiration, vision, and design for Cowboys Stadium in this new age. And this is a very different age.

Jerry Jones
Owner, Dallas Cowboys

Big is a relative term, even when it comes to stadiums. The word "stadium" originates from the Greek term "stadion", a measure of length roughly 180 to 200 meters, the distance of an ancient sprinting competition. The first stadiums, like the one at Olympia, Greece, where the earliest Olympic Games of antiquity were held, were not much larger than that. While elaborate for their time, by today's standards they were relatively simple structures, essentially elaborate stone bleachers. The new Cowboys Stadium stretches a quarter of a mile in length, enclosing 3 million square feet. The Statue of Liberty can stand up inside the roof structure. It is an immense volume, containing roughly 104 million cubic feet of space. The seats (there are over 80,000 of them, with flexibility to reach over 100,000) are elegant, many comfortably padded, with excellent views of the field. If for some reason you don't want to enjoy that view, a colossal high-definition television screen hangs almost the entire length of the field.

It would be an understatement to say that stadiums have changed physically over the course of history. Their essential role in culture, however, has not changed. Stadiums provide one of the greatest expressions of communal drama conceived by civilization. We congregate in church to be intimate with our God. We proceed en masse to vote, and privately elect those who will lead us. We go to sports stadiums to see humanity at its highest point of physical achievement, and to scream our bloody heads off at those who perform our own unfulfilled desires. Call it primitive, but the crude act of those guttural expressions feels innately good, and makes even the timid express themselves in surprising ways. To see a ninety-year-old grandmother with a Cowboys star painted on her forehead is to understand that this need is a part of the genetic makeup of humanity. To be part of a stadium crowd is an ancient ritual of inspiration.

The twenty-first century, however, is a new ball game. Stadiums are not just about sports, but entertainment in the grandest sense. Those of us old enough to have seen television coverage in the 1960s of The Beatles at Shea Stadium remember thinking that not only had music changed, but the concept of "the stage" had changed, as well. If sports stadiums provided big entertainment in the past, they had the potential of becoming mega, multimedia entertainment centers. That reality is here, and it has arrived in the form of what looks like a monumental steel and glass spaceship. This isn't just a big new building. It is a form of postmodern architecture: part arena, part sleek minimalist sculpture. If the role of

OPPOSITE Viewed through the fritted glass curtain wall, a monumental steel arch soars skyward.

architecture is to send a message, this Star Trek-like structure points to an unknown future. Driving along Interstate 30, it can be seen from miles away, and we wonder just what exactly it will bring to this planet of ours. Jerry Jones has a simple answer: "Anything that is exciting and entertaining."

Indeed, Jones, an Arkansas oilman who purchased a struggling Dallas Cowboys football team with a handshake deal and 140 million dollars in 1989, has not only brought his team back to serious contention, but has also now conceived a new vision of stadium entertainment. When he and his family initially fantasized building a new stadium, they imagined their world-recognized sports franchise as part of an even broader collage that would include not only multiple sports events other than football, but music, theater, and art. But the Cowboys are the most successful sports franchise in history, and one of the most marketable brands worldwide, so why the other stuff? "Of the millions of fans who follow the NFL around the world," Jones has said, "only seven percent of them ever attend a game in a stadium. We are grateful that television brings the game to a larger audience, but we want to bring more people into the tent. If that means rethinking the concept of a sports stadium, we're ready to do that."

In a sports business typically known for its narrow focus, the supersized capacity of the new Cowboys Stadium is a reflection of an unusually expansive thought process. Is the suggestion that a sports stadium can capture the interest of a wide-ranging audience, even those that are not football fans, simply rhetoric? Jones says no. "It's not rhetoric. It's the future." It is a future where the boundaries of sports, entertainment, and the arts are blended into a remarkably broad creative platform. In its first year the new stadium has presented, along with football, internationally recognized soccer, boxing, and basketball competitions. It has also hosted performances by George Strait and Reba McEntire, the Jonas Brothers, Paul McCartney, U2, and *American Idol* auditions, as well as special symphonic events. The Jones "team," including Jerry; his wife, Gene; daughter, Charlotte; and sons, Stephen and Jerry Jr., seem to discuss matters of stadium programming 24/7, contemplating a cultural reach between Professional Bull Riders and Monster Energy Supercross to classical music and theater. The Cowboys Stadium suggests a populist version of the famous cultural fantasy the Germans call a *Gesamtkunstwerk*, translated as an all-embracing synthesis of the arts—a "total work of art."

Besides its popular appeal, the new stadium has engaged the cutting edge of culture as well. One of the most innovative aspects of the Cowboys' new home is its program of contemporary art. While most stadium owners are content to place a few sports photographs and bronze statues of players around in discreet little niches, the Jones family has stepped outside the box, enveloping their visitors with wall murals and hanging sculpture. The often bland, concrete walls of the typical stadium have become canvases for some of the world's most daring and inventive artists. Many of the works were commissioned as the building was still in construction,

The twenty-first century . . . is a new ball game. Stadiums are not just about sports, but entertainment in the grandest sense.

MICHAEL AUPING

leaving the final outcome of the interaction between the architecture and the art unknown until the building opened in 2009. Gene Jones, the instigator of the implausible idea of putting world-class art in a football stadium, has said, "We felt that contemporary art has become much more a part of what people talk about these days. We don't think it is just for an elite group of people, so why not think about bringing it in? The fact that this was a boundary that other sports venues had definitely not crossed probably attracted us to it more, particularly Jerry." The Joneses are either very smart, lucky, or both. By all accounts the commissioned series of works at Cowboys Stadium has quickly become one of the finest examples of contemporary public art in the world. When you hear the comment that the new Cowboys Stadium is "state of the art," you can believe it. It does what many contemporary art museums have a difficult time doing—presenting cutting-edge art to a broad public. Perhaps the Joneses, who have only recently become involved with contemporary art, knew that if you strip away the elite façade of the art museum and place a new idea or image in an unexpected place—a stadium?!—it can be seen with new eyes.

A surprising result of this unusual combination is the interplay between the art and the action on the field. The Jones family's leap of faith has inspired the artists to compete for our attention just as the players do on the field. These are not cute little decorations timidly hovering in the background. At different entrances, elegant, minimalist sculptures draw visitors' eyes around the ceilings and walls of the cavernous space. Above concession stands, abstract lines of color create illusions that torque the architecture as if it were a giant sheet of paper. In another area, a black wall is shattered by hundreds of mirrored pieces of glass and aluminum. The 21 pieces in the collection occupy nearly 100,000 square feet of space. This is more square footage devoted to art than most major contemporary art museums. As someone who has frequented sports events, concerts, and museums over many years, I can say with some authority that there is nothing like this anywhere in the world.

The concept behind this new stadium is surely no surprise to other team owners. They are well aware that the Jones family has a track record for marketing innovation. They have not only kept the Cowboys in the upper echelon of sports franchises, but they have been mavericks in aggressively marketing their team, at times butting heads with the indomitable NFL itself. They have been criticized, and later copied, for their bold moves to make the Cowboys an independent global brand. They are now marketing an even broader and more inclusive experience.

The stadiums that line roads from Greece to Texas encompass a long and fascinating history, and as with all histories there have been special moments when a particular time requires a new form. This stadium will surely be an example of such a time. The tent just got much bigger and more beautiful.

Michael Auping, Chief Curator,
Modern Art Museum of Fort Worth

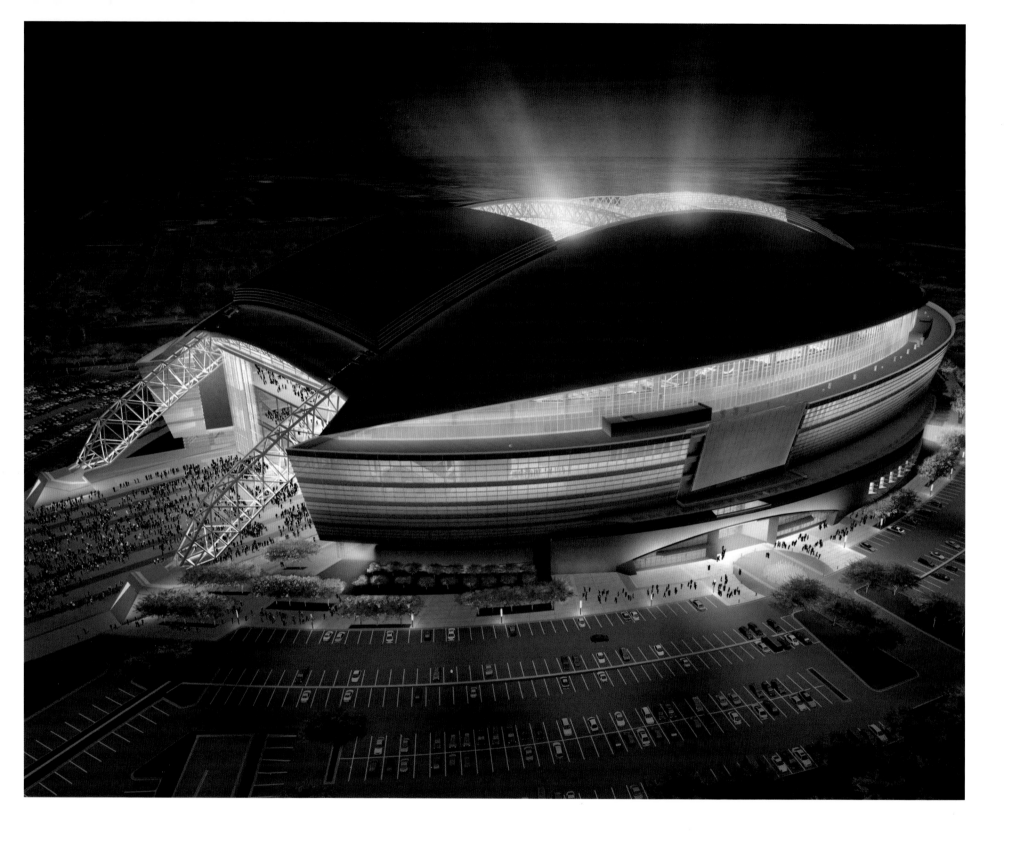

ARCHITECTURE

A GRAND VISION: AN INNOVATIVE APPROACH TO ARCHITECTURE AND ENTERTAINMENT

By David Dillon

Picture a flat-screen TV, a sleek, high-definition electronic abstraction like the one in your family room. And then imagine it enlarged 2,000 times its normal size and suspended from a football stadium roof so that you and 100,000 other fans have close-up, unobstructed views of gigantic padded and helmeted figures sprinting up and down a green rectangle like creatures out of *Jurassic Park*.

To those who find it strange to pay $100 to watch an NFL game on a huge video screen that you could watch at home for free, Dallas Cowboys owner Jerry Jones replies, "Here comes the future." The Cowboys' main competition these days, he insists, is not the Redskins or the Giants but the home media center.

"Only seven percent of NFL fans have been inside an NFL stadium. Why is that, when we're the most popular sport? Our challenge is to compete and win the home entertainment battle by offering a product that fans can't experience at home, yet using the technology they do have at home."

Thus, a 160-foot-wide-by-72-foot-high digital media board, the biggest, most expensive ever, hovering like the starship *Enterprise* over the center of the field. Compared to it, the digital scoreboards in basketball and hockey arenas look like postage stamps.

Jerry Jones says he first realized the potential of this technology during a Céline Dion concert in Las Vegas, during which the stylish French-Canadian chanteuse performed on a conventional stage backed by a huge video screen that magnified every facial expression and hand gesture.

"I can't remember if I was watching her or watching the screen," says Jones, "but I had never seen anything so dynamic."

The mega video board has generated so much fan buzz that it now competes with the star and the hole in the old stadium roof as the team icon. At the same time it is about more than the Cowboys, more than football. It is the symbol of the stadium as a year-round, multifaceted twenty-first-century entertainment machine where rock concerts, bull riding, prizefights, and monster trucks will get equal billing. For Jerry Jones, the video board represents a sports communication revolution as different from what has gone before as *Avatar* is from a black-and-white movie.

Breaking New Ground

Jerry Jones is known as a bold entrepreneur and a brilliant marketer, yet until the debut of Cowboys Stadium in 2009 nobody thought of him or his family as serious art and architecture patrons. To some diehard Cowboys they were still Arkansas outsiders, who rolled into town in 1989 and wrested control of one of the world's premiere sports franchises from native Texans.

"That perception of our family that many had was never right," says daughter Charlotte Anderson. "People assumed we didn't know what we were doing. That put a lot of pressure on us to get [the stadium] right so that when people walked in, they'd say, 'It's so much better than we ever imagined.'"

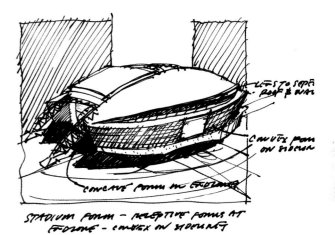

OPPOSITE The stadium at night as shown in an HKS rendering mirrors the look of the completed stadium.

ABOVE An HKS sketch shows the relationship between the form of the roofline and the slope of the glass curtain wall.

Ever since his days as a guard on the University of Arkansas football team in the early 1960s (which also included future Cowboys coach Jimmy Johnson), Jerry Jones has wanted to immerse himself in football—as a player, scout, coach, and eventually an owner. He bought the Cowboys in 1989 for $140 million, leveraging most of his oil and gas fortune to close the deal. This was a hefty sum to pay for a mediocre team that was hemorrhaging money, a bad business decision in the opinion of many friends. So he decided to make the Cowboys a family operation, with no investors and partners other than his wife and their three children, Stephen, Charlotte, and Jerry Jr. Having worked in his father's insurance and grocery businesses as a young man, he was not leaping into the unknown.

The division of labor on the stadium was straightforward: Jerry the big-picture guy, "our Walt Disney" to his family; Gene watching over design details, from the curve of the roof (she thought the first version looked too much like a turtle's shell) to the pattern of the crystal and china in the club dining room; Stephen, Charlotte, and Jerry Jr. looking after money, special events and marketing, respectively.

Like many family businesses, the Cowboys organization is close-knit, self-protective, and at times fiercely competitive.

"I had five bosses and they weren't always pulling in the same directions," recalls John Dixon, who coordinated the stadium project for Manhattan Construction Company. "We'd sometimes meet for days about this point and that, but in the end everyone came to a decision and that was that."

Predictably, Jerry has a punchier version. "First we'd exchange points of view, then we'd debate, and if that didn't get it done, we'd argue."

Between 2004, when design began, and 2009, when the stadium finally opened, the budget doubled from $650 million to $1.2 billion. Though known as a tough bargainer who can wring every dollar out of every deal, on the stadium Jerry Jones said yes far more often than he said no.

"Usually it's the parents who tell their children not to spend so much money," says Gene with a smile, "but in this case our own kids were telling *us* not to do it."

ABOVE LEFT The historic Colosseum in Rome.

ABOVE RIGHT Foster + Partners–designed Wembley Stadium in London, England.

ABOVE LEFT Herzog & de Meuron–
designed Allianz Arena in
Munich, Germany.

ABOVE RIGHT Herzog & de Meuron–
designed Beijing National Stadium,
also known as the Bird's Nest, and was
home to the 2008 Summer Olympics.

Before it was over, Jerry would approve an additional $40 million to $50 million for the video board, $20 million to upgrade the outdoor plazas, $10 million for wider concourses, and many times that amount on a limestone base, fritted glass walls, and double-height glass entrances on the north and south. He's often said that he spent $400 million on the stadium that he didn't have to.

"When you're in charge of the Dallas Cowboys, one of the most valuable sports franchises in the world, and you have a chance to add to that value, you have to do it. You aren't just building a place where people come to sit and grin at one another but something for 15 or 20 years from now."

Searching for Architecture and an Architect

In buying the Dallas Cowboys, Jerry Jones also inherited Texas Stadium in suburban Irving, home to five Super Bowl championship teams but architecturally strictly utilitarian. The 1960s were a bad decade for sports architecture—and most other kinds of architecture as well—as the elegant structural refinements of Mies van der Rohe, Eero Saarinen, and other postwar modernists devolved into a cheerless, "take that" Brutalism in which polemic became more important than people. Most stadiums of this era were barebones steel and concrete enclosures designed for football and baseball but ideal for neither. The New York Jets and the Pittsburgh Steelers played in such venues, as did the Philadelphia Eagles, Oakland Raiders, and half a dozen other teams. Exciting architecture was not part of the program.

Texas Stadium was different in being for football only and one of the first to include exclusive private suites. It had been designed by Dallas architect A. Warren Morey for the Cowboys' first owner, Clint Murchison Jr., who believed that football was gladiatorial combat and should be presented that way. Fans might have been entitled to a few amenities, a bit of shade perhaps, but players were expected to slug it out in rain, snow, and scorching sun. Thus, the roof with the hole in the center, a beacon for planes coming into Dallas/Fort Worth International Airport as well as a way to avoid air-conditioning, which even in the era of $3-per-barrel oil cost a bunch. Suites were Murchison's major concession to luxury, and, at $50,000 and up, plus tickets, for an unfinished

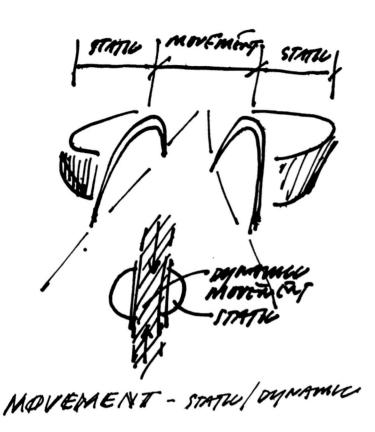

STATIC | MOVEMENT | STATIC

DYNAMIC
MOVEMENT
STATIC

MOVEMENT - STATIC/DYNAMIC

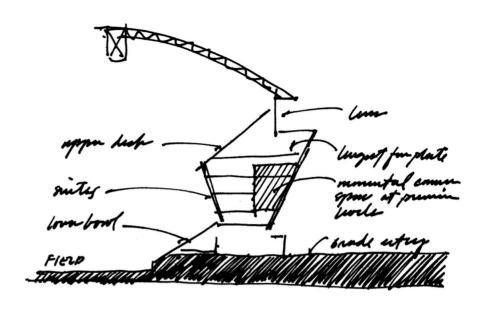

upper deck

suites

lower bowl

FIELD

luxury floor plate

monumental common space at premium levels

grade entry

SECTION C SIDELINE - form responds to need for more floor plate at top.

COWBOYS 11. OCT. 2001

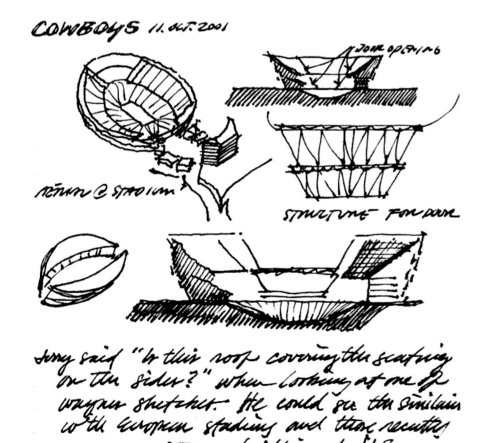

JOINT OPENING

return @ stadium

STRUCTURE FOR DOOR

Jerry said "Is this roof covering the seating on the sides?" when looking at one of Wayne's sketches. He could see the similarity to European stadiums and those recently built in the U.S.

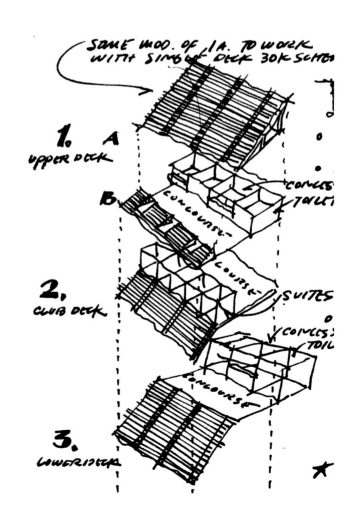

SOME MOD. OF 1A. TO WORK WITH SINGLE DECK 30K SUITES

1. A
UPPER DECK
B
CONCOURSE TOILET

2.
CLUB DECK
CONCOURSE
SUITES
CONCOURSE TOIL

3.
LOWER DECK
CONCOURSE

When the time came to build a new stadium, Jerry Jones would make it everything that Texas Stadium was not: multidimensional, technologically sophisticated, and air-conditioned.

DAVID DILLON

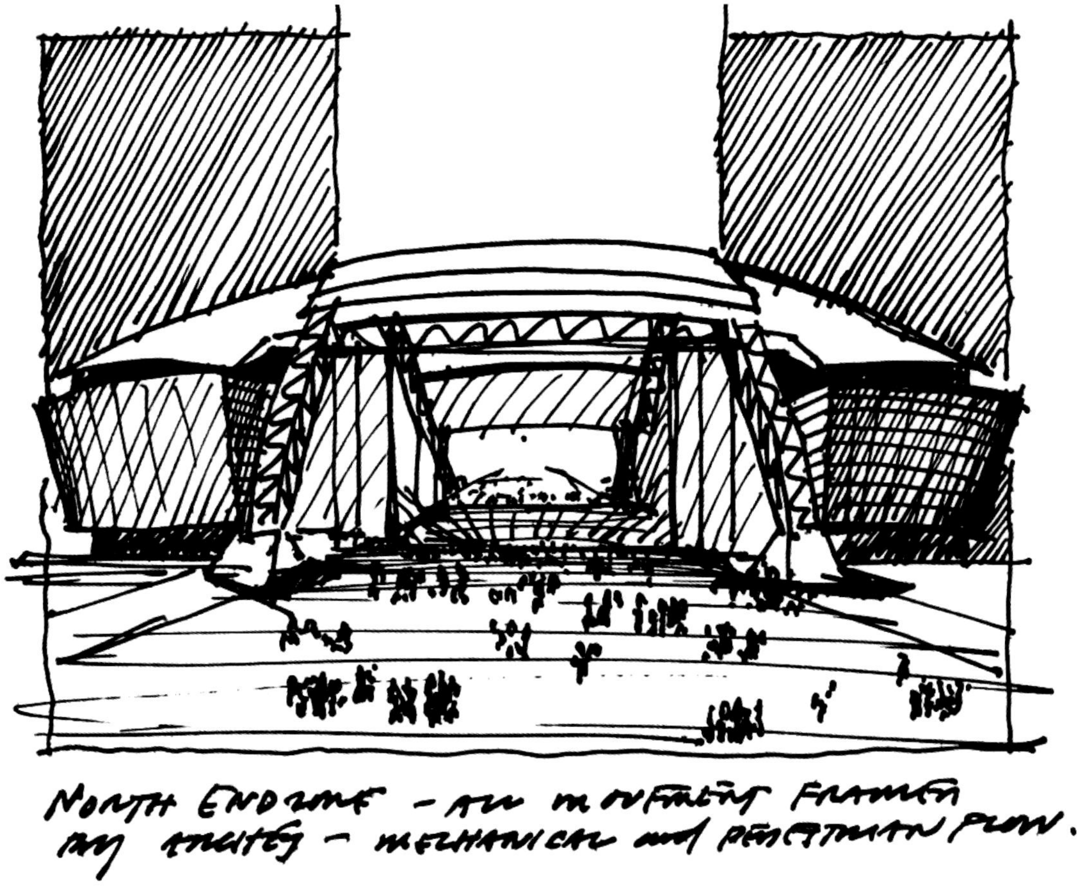

OPPOSITE Preliminary HKS sketches show the evolution of movement, form, and function in the stadium's design.

ABOVE An early HKS depiction of the open end-zone platforms, as viewed from the plaza.

shell were bargain-basement cheap compared to $1 million and up with tickets for completed suites in the new stadium.

No sooner had he bought the team than Jerry Jones started thinking about renovating Texas Stadium, only to conclude that he'd still have an antiquated facility with no additional seating, no air-conditioning, and no flexibility in accommodating other kinds of events. Economically, Texas Stadium was a non-starter; architecturally it was a reverse inspiration. When the time came to build a new stadium, he would make it everything that Texas Stadium was not: multidimensional, technologically sophisticated, and air-conditioned.

Becoming Good Clients

Gene and Jerry Jones acknowledge that when the stadium project began in 2001 they knew little about contemporary art and architecture. They lived in a traditional 1920s Mediterranean house in Highland Park that had been tastefully renovated by Dallas architect Cole Smith; they owned a handful of Norman Rockwell paintings, along with considerable sports art and memorabilia. But they were not serious collectors who, like many members of their social circle, had spent years and fortunes acquiring major works by leading contemporary

We knew we didn't want everything to be stars & Cowboys blue. We wanted something so that even if you weren't a Cowboys fan you'd enjoy the stadium.

GENE JONES

artists and installing them in houses designed by Richard Meier, I. M. Pei, Antoine Predock, and other celebrity architects.

"We knew we didn't want everything to be stars and Cowboys blue," Gene recalls. "We wanted something so that even if you weren't a Cowboys fan you'd enjoy the stadium. But we had to decide what that meant."

And so, with an enthusiasm that perhaps only novices can muster, they set out to become good clients instead of merely passive consumers. They read, traveled, and followed the suggestions of thoughtful architects. Gene was asked to join the board of the future Dallas Center for the Performing Arts, where she met Rem Koolhaas and Sir Norman Foster, the eventual winners of the Center's $355 million competition. She hosted both of them at a dinner at her home, and later met with Foster and also toured his new Wembley Stadium in London. They also traveled to Rome, Paris, Berlin, and Beijing, boxing the architectural compass from ancient monuments to cutting-edge designs.

In August 2001, the Cowboys organized a design competition that would extend over several months, with the final round held in Wichita Falls, Texas, the team's preseason training camp. Participating were HOK Sports of Kansas City, NBBJ from Seattle,

1. Entry A

Guests enter at this main year-round entrance to the stadium. The signature design element is the sweeping 224-foot arch, detailed with stainless steel plating, flanked by illuminated glass panels.

2. American Airlines Lounge/Sony Lounge

These clubs on opposite sides of the stadium feature a 3-story open atrium with floor-to-ceiling windows, providing an abundance of natural light. This space is exclusive to suite owners and club seat patrons.

3. Pro Shop

The 13,000 square-foot, multi-level Pro Shop, located just inside the main entrance, offers every visitor a unique shopping experience.

4. Suites

Plush leather seats, private full-service bar, flat-screen televisions and a private restroom are just a few of the features in the luxury suites. Removable glass panels open the entire space to the playing field.

5. Main Concourse Club

At 33,000 square-feet, the main concourse clubs are the largest in the stadium. These five-star clubs are designed with style and comfort in mind, featuring private bars and upscale dining options.

6. End-zone Platforms

The flexibility of the six open end-zone decks provide sweeping vistas unique to the stadium while allowing the venue's capacity to expand to over 100,000 fans.

7. Field Suites

Found only at Cowboys Stadium, these field level sideline suites, complete with private patios, offer access to clubs by which the players enter the field.

8. The Field

Cowboys Stadium has three separate synthetic fields for NFL football, college and high school football, and a blank field that can be painted to accommodate any other sport.

9. Dallas Cowboys Locker Room

The Dallas Cowboys locker room features custom-built lockers, a modern athletic training room, equipment room, and x-ray facilities. The coaching staff has its own locker room within this space.

10. High-Def Digital Media Board

A 1.2 million-pound digital media board is suspended from the ceiling, 90 feet above the playing field. The two sideline screens measure 72 feet in height and 160 feet in length, the largest in the world.

11. Roof

Reminiscent of the signature roof at Texas Stadium, Cowboys Stadium has a domed top with two retractable fabric panels that can open or close in 12 minutes to cover the opening above the field.

12. Ring of Honor

From Bob Lilly to the "Triplets" of Troy Aikman, Michael Irvin, and Emmitt Smith, the 17 Cowboys greats forever have their names commemorated on the wall above the playing field.

13. End-zone Doors

The ends of the stadium feature five retractable glass panels 120 feet in height, the largest movable glass walls in the world. These doors open in eight minutes to create a 180-foot-wide entry from the plazas.

14. Arches

The quarter-mile arches do more than support the retractable roof. Using arches instead of interior columns reduces the number of obstructed view seats while providing structural support for the digital media board.

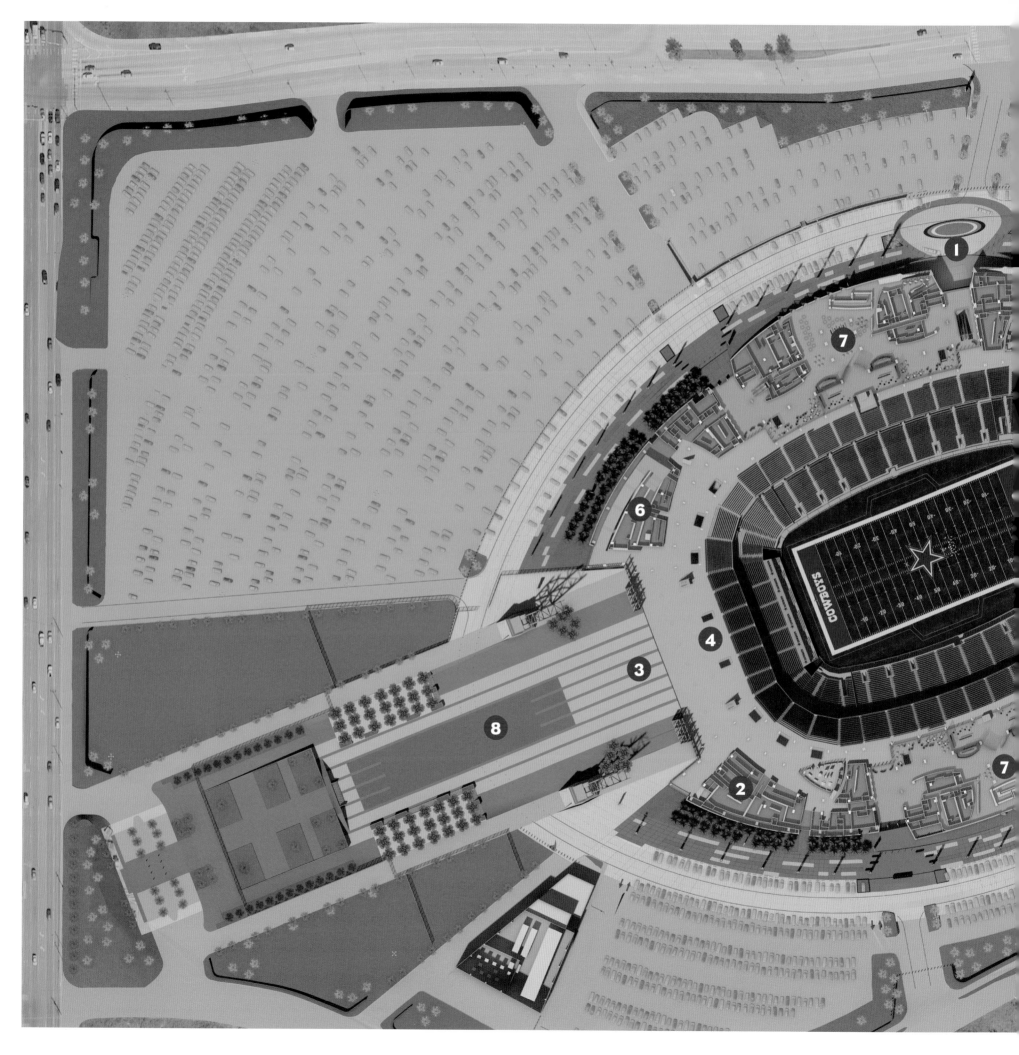

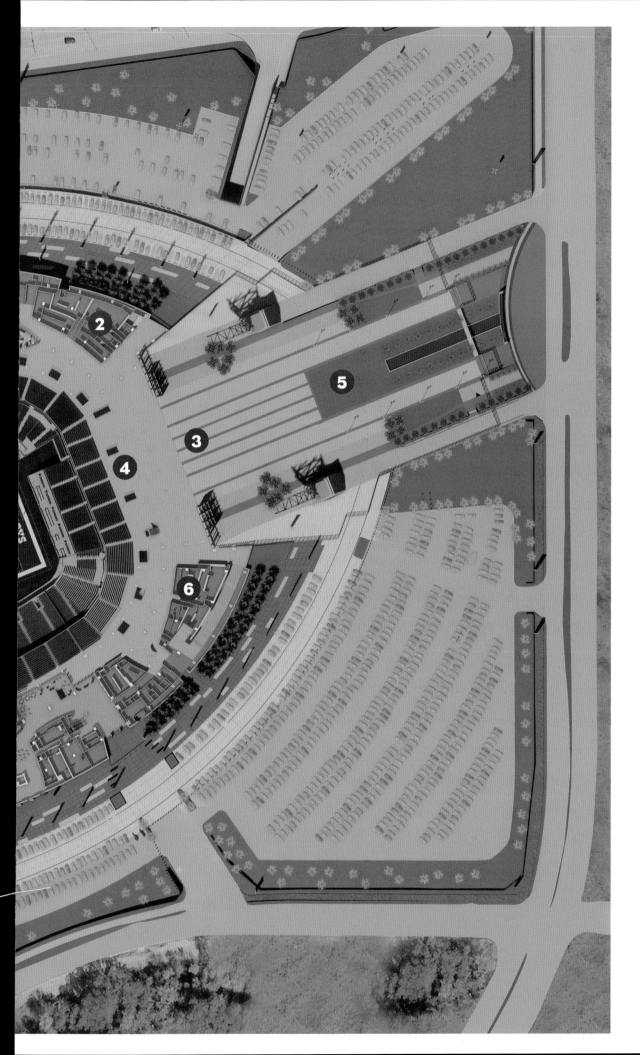

and HKS in Dallas. The first two were established sports architecture firms with major stadiums and arenas around the country. HKS, on the other hand, was a newcomer, having previously renovated suites at Texas Stadium in the 1990s, and been architect of record for the American Airlines Center in Dallas, home of the NBA Mavericks and NHL Stars, and the Texas Rangers Ballpark in Arlington. But HKS had never designed a stadium from scratch. Bryan Trubey and his team were all in their twenties and thirties. Within HKS, one of the largest architecture firms in the country, the sports group was barely visible compared to the hugely profitable health care and office building divisions. The stadium competition was the group's chance to break into the big time, to show what it could do on its own and on a grand scale.

The final round lasted an entire day, with each firm presenting models, plans, and drawings, and Jerry Jones acting as critic-in-residence. Considering that he was dangling one of the richest sports commissions in modern times, he could probably have hired any architect he wanted. But what he wanted more than a superstar was an architect who would take his ideas seriously. He also wanted to be part of the process, involved in every major decision, which would have been impossible with architects based in London or Paris.

At the end of the day Jerry Jones chose HKS, not for their marquee value, obviously, but because he knew their work, they were right next door, and because their edgy, unconventional ideas appealed to his "push the limits" personality. He sensed they were a firm on the rise.

"Jerry operates a lot on gut feeling," says Trubey. "He could see that we were passionate about the project and would put everything we had into it."

Searching for a Home

Commission in hand, HKS started in on a schematic design for the new stadium, the basic themes of which they had articulated in the competition: transparency, flexibility, and the latest technology, meaning a retractable roof and end-zone doors, and state-of-the art communications equipment, though the idea for the *coup de grâce* video board was still several years away.

Yet without a site, progress on the schematic design vacillated between episodic and glacial. Instead of sitting at their computers and drafting boards, Trubey and his HKS team spent much of their time in a helicopter, scouting possible sites. They studied some two dozen locations around North Texas, including Irving, Grapevine, Duncanville, and Dallas. There they focused on a riverfront site downtown, before shifting to Fair Park, a national historic landmark surrounded by a depressed minority neighborhood desperately in need of investment. The Cowboys

proposed a year-round sports and entertainment district that included a museum, shops, restaurants, and rides, all anchored by a $650 million stadium funded jointly by the team and Dallas County through a hotel/motel and car rental tax.

The Cowboys touted the stadium as a boon to tourism and development, at the same time reminding Dallas that archrival Houston had lassoed the 2004 Super Bowl by delivering a new stadium. City and county officials worried that the project would hurt convention business and increase the tax rate. Dallas leaders said flat out that they would rather put $325 million into revitalizing downtown than into football.

Negotiations went nowhere, with the parties unable to find enough common ground for an agreement. In June 2004 the Cowboys called it quits and decamped for Arlington, a sprawling suburb midway between Dallas and Fort Worth that was already a sports and entertainment destination because of the Texas Rangers ballpark, Six Flags Over Texas, and other popular attractions. There, Mayor Robert Cluck and other city officials welcomed the stadium as an economic bonanza that would put Arlington on the international sports map.

In November 2004, despite heated opposition, Arlington voters approved the new stadium by a 55 to 45 percent margin, with the city and the team agreeing to split the $650 million bill. The Cowboys ran a high-powered, shrewdly orchestrated campaign that included appearances and endorsements by former stars Roger

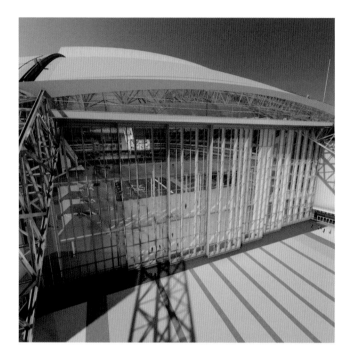

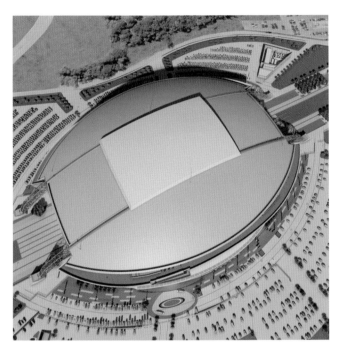

OPPOSITE TOP The 180-foot-wide-by-120-foot-high operable glass end-zone doors are located at each end of the stadium.

OPPOSITE BOTTOM Through the architects' use of clear glass for the door panels, spectators experience panoramic views from within the seating bowl and end-zone platforms.

TOP When closed, the roof encompasses 104 million cubic feet, making it the largest enclosed NFL stadium.

BOTTOM The retractable roof recalls the signature opening at Texas Stadium.

Staubach, Troy Aikman, and Emmitt Smith. Ironically, the least visible Cowboy of all was Jerry Jones, who chose to stay on the sidelines rather than be a target for opponent barbs. "There have been more sightings of J.D. Salinger in recent weeks than Jerry Jones," quipped one news reporter.

Simple Dynamic Forms

Arlington being Arlington, and Jerry Jones being Jerry Jones, there was plenty of street talk that the new stadium would be another nostalgic period piece like the Texas Rangers ballpark. But as happened frequently over the next several years, the speculators were wrong. Reading and traveling and talking with top designers had given Gene and Jerry a broader understanding of architectural possibilities. When they were on the road, Bryan Trubey fired off e-mails and faxes suggesting buildings to visit, including Herzog & de Meuron's Allianz Arena in Munich, with its silvery, transparent skin, and Cesar Pelli's Bloomberg headquarters in New York, a shimmering glass tower with crisp stainless-steel fins that cast intriguing shadow patterns on the façade. These visits amounted to a crash course in contemporary forms and materials, and would prove extremely valuable as the design of Cowboys Stadium evolved.

"Football is tough and cutting-edge and about the future," says Gene. "The stadium had to be contemporary, with contemporary art."

For every rendering we did on an ordinary building we must have done 100 for this one. We probably did 50 for the glass wall alone.

BRYAN TRUBEY

This fit Bryan Trubey's program for a building that was formally simple but functionally complex. The combination of strong forms and elegant proportions would also allow him to spend more money on materials and finishes and less on fussy decorative effects.

Strong forms meant soaring steel arches, curved and canted glass walls, a retractable roof with a translucent skin, and monumental glass doors at the ends for views and cross ventilation. These basic elements came together quickly, in three or four months, but the details seemed to take forever.

"For every rendering we did on an ordinary building, we must have done 100 for this one," Trubey says. "We probably did 50 for the glass wall alone."

Even the quest for something as ordinary as epoxy for floors and baseboards took on Homeric proportions, with Jerry Jones dragging friends and family to airport terminals, shopping centers, even neighbors' garages, to ferret out the quintessential finish. Everyone involved has an epoxy story. "It became our four-letter word," says Charlotte.

Arches are timeless expressions of strength and grace, the essence of doing more with less. The two at Cowboys Stadium are made of high-grade steel imported from Luxembourg, fabricated in Oklahoma, and trucked to Arlington. They span 1,225 feet, the longest single spans ever built, and extend beyond the stadium's end walls to massive steel and concrete abutments that transfer roof loads

ABOVE Construction began with the excavation of 1.6 million cubic yards of dirt as the stadium floor was established 50 feet below grade.

OPPOSITE Soaring nearly 300 feet, shoring towers support the monumental steel arches during the early stages of construction.

into deep underground trenches. Simultaneously feats of structural engineering and monumental industrial sculptures, these arches recall those that appeared briefly in early renderings of Texas Stadium, as though they had been in hiding, waiting for a second chance.

Simpler and cheaper structural solutions existed, such as jumbo corner columns like those in the Arizona Cardinals stadium in Phoenix—a Jerry Jones favorite—and Lucas Oil Stadium in Indianapolis, which HKS designed for the Colts. Corner columns mean shorter spans, less steel, and potentially big savings.

"We could have saved a lot of money if we had done that, or just put the arches inside the building," says David Platten, a structural engineer with Walter P. Moore, Inc. of Dallas, who was on site from day one.

But Jerry Jones wasn't buying it. Clean horizontal lines and a taut skin said "modern" and "progressive" to him, and he was willing to pay for it. "He got the idea immediately," says Trubey. "There was no argument."

The basic form of the roof was mostly Jerry's as well. At 661,000 square feet, it is the largest roof of its kind in the world, and mechanically one of the most complicated. Retractable roofs are usually flat and horizontal, whereas the Cowboys' version slopes upward 23 degrees, distributing its massive loads laterally as well as straight down—thus the stabilizing underground trenches and the complicated rack-and-pinion system for opening and closing the roof panels.

Hanging the video board was equally daunting—1.2 million pounds, plus 200,000 pounds of stage rigging, all suspended from steel trusses 90 feet above the playing field. Platten remembers the experience as "fascinating and weird at the same time, like floating a ten-story building in midair."

Light is the Theme

The quest for light, clarity, and transparency drove the stadium's design from the beginning. Though the building contains three million square feet, you rarely lose contact with the outside world. The retractable roof is covered in a translucent Teflon-coated material that admits 12 percent of the available natural light. Even on cloudy days you tend to forget that you're indoors. Light also enters through a clerestory just below the roofline, as well as through monumental retractable doors in both end zones. When open, these 120-by-180-foot nesting doors bring air and light deep into the seating bowl; when closed, they serve as giant picture windows that frame the

LEFT An abutment—25 feet wide—provides the foundation and support for the bearing pin assembly for an arch truss.

MIDDLE The installation of the first section of arch truss.

RIGHT The completion of the first segment of arch truss, each 17 feet wide and 35 feet deep.

OPPOSITE LEFT The arched truss under construction, supported by shoring towers.

OPPOSITE MIDDLE The north arch truss as it nears completion.

OPPOSITE RIGHT The north arch truss completes a quarter mile long span.

surrounding landscape; at night they become huge mirrors that reflect the swirl of activity on the outdoor plazas.

The light theme also appears, at a different scale, in the two smaller side entrances on the north and south. Gene Jones felt that both were too low and cramped, so on the southern entrance—known to everyone as "Gene's entrance"—she insisted on doubling the height of the outside doors as well as eliminating an interior glass partition. The revised version is more cubic and crystalline, and allows fans a nearly unobstructed view of the seating bowl the moment they walk through the door.

On the northern, or "365," entrance, so called because it is open every day of the year, Gene orchestrated a collaboration between Bryan Trubey and her own residential architect, Cole Smith. He proposed a series of tall, slender arches, which after much discussion evolved into a gentle, welcoming curve that is more architecturally consistent with the rest of the stadium. The ribbed stainless steel ceiling was inspired by a small Cartier compact from Gene's dressing room table at home—a decorative arts touch for a sleek contemporary space.

Connecting the sloping roof and the limestone base are two curving fritted glass walls, each 900 feet long with a 14-degree cant that plays against the stadium's powerful horizontals. The frit, a pattern of tiny dots on the glass, transitions from 90 percent coverage at the bottom to only 10 percent near the top, giving the stadium as many moods as the day—shadowy in the morning, sparkling in the midday sun, lantern-like in the evening. Pilots approaching Dallas/Fort Worth International now navigate by it the way they previously used the hole in the Texas Stadium roof.

As emphatically as any single element, the fritted glass walls highlight the continuity between the stadium's interior and exterior. In most recent stadiums—the Ballpark in Arlington, Minute Maid Park in Houston, Coors Field in Denver—the façade is essentially a wrapper, a bit of packaging, that has little to do with what's going on inside. This wrapper is often designed by a second architect, whose job it is to create a look or an image while leaving function to others. At Cowboys Stadium, on the other hand, form and function are tightly integrated: what you see outside is basically what you get inside. Materials, structure, geometry, and finishes all carry through from one to another, creating a more or less seamless whole derived from a coherent architectural idea.

Burnishing the Brand

In building Cowboys Stadium, Jerry Jones discovered that good architecture is also good marketing. One of his heroes is Walt Disney, who tweaked and refined the image of Mickey Mouse to the point that it became a universal brand. "When he built Disneyland nobody in the country had to ask where it was or what it was about," he says enviously. "We'd all been brainwashed."

Keeping the hole in the stadium roof was a nod in that direction, a reminder of the Cowboys' glory days. But in reading and traveling, he and Gene also saw how leading international companies had used contemporary architecture to show clients that they were in the know instead of behind the curve. Seagram commissioned Mies van der Rohe to design its landmark tower on Park Avenue; IBM turned to Skidmore Owings & Merrill and others for its offices and factories. Rem Koolhaas dressed up Prada's image; Frank Gehry did the same for Vitra, the German furniture manufacturer. The Dallas Cowboys were already an international brand, one of the most recognized names in professional sports; Jerry's marketing antennae told him that bold contemporary architecture, suggestive of innovation and the future, could only enhance it. "He's brilliant at intuiting intangible value, or the value of the intangible," notes Bryan Trubey. "Our job was to turn that intuition into architecture."

LEFT The assembly of the support structure for the 1.2 million-pound digital media board, on the floor of the stadium.

MIDDLE A worker installs one of the video display modules, which measures approximately 4 1/2 feet tall by 6 feet wide.

RIGHT The 160-foot-wide-by-72-foot-high digital media board is suspended 90 feet above the playing surface.

ABOVE The interior of the video board has ten levels of catwalks, accessed from the field through one of two remote-controlled lifts.

Instead of slogging from car to gate to seat, fans would pass groves of magnolias & live oak trees with benches, fountains, and panels of lawn for picnics or simply soaking up the excitement of the moment.

DAVID DILLON

Grand Settings for Grand Events

Cowboys Stadium was going to be supersized. Jerry Jones and Texans' contempt for understatement took care of that. Three million square feet, one-third bigger than any other contemporary stadium, with up to 100,000 seats for special events such as the Super Bowl and the NBA All-Star Game, which drew a record 108,000 fans in February 2010. Its scale rivals that of the stadiums and coliseums of Greece and Rome, a comparison not lost on the Cowboy's public relations staff, which managed to work it into promotions and press releases at every opportunity.

Bryan Trubey spent weeks studying these ancient precedents, less as sources of specific architectural details than as settings for grand public events. A missing element in most contemporary stadiums is a sense of ceremony and arrival, that feeling that you are about to experience something special and memorable. Typically they float in a sea of parking, their entrances dammed by bumpers, beer stands, and shabby commercial advertising. Trubey wanted the approaches to Cowboys Stadium to be different, with long axial views that say, "This is an important building." So, collaborating with Dallas landscape architects Roland Jackson and Paul Fields, he designed two monumental plazas on the east and west ends of the stadium, one measuring 600 feet by 300 feet, the other 600 feet by 900 feet. Instead

of slogging from car to gate to seat, fans would pass groves of magnolias and live oak trees with benches, fountains, and panels of lawn for picnics or simply soaking up the excitement of moment. They would enter through monumental doorways, contemporary versions of ancient triumphal arches, into a vast light-filled stadium. And because the bowl sits 50 feet below grade they would enter on the main concourse level, then walk down or up to their seats. After the event they could mill about among performers and vendors, watching game highlights on huge screens or just hanging out as in an impromptu open-air bazaar.

Sixty percent of fans now enter the stadium through these ceremonial plazas, for which Brian Trubey credits Gene and her daughter, Charlotte. They returned from the 2008 Olympics in Beijing awed by the structural brilliance of Herzog & de Meuron's "Bird's Nest," but determined not to replicate the vast concrete expanses in and around it. "It was a magnificent structure that lacked the finishes and level of intimacy that we were looking for," says Charlotte.

Inside the stadium Cowboys fans will find not only beer, nachos, team gear, and bobblehead dolls of their favorite players, but also big, bold pieces of contemporary art that can't be ignored. (See David Pagel's essay, page 65) Franz Ackermann's gigantic murals, *Coming Home* and *(Meet me) At the Waterfall*, wrap the main staircase in movement and color.

ABOVE Sun dances off the stadium's reflecting pool and glass end-zone doors.

ABOVE The graceful curve of the monumental steel arches silhouetted in the evening sky.

LEFT Fireworks explode high above Cowboys Stadium.

RIGHT A granite fountain at Entry F
complements the steel and glass of the
exterior curtain wall.

LEFT The steel arch design of the roof is replicated above the stadium's main entry.

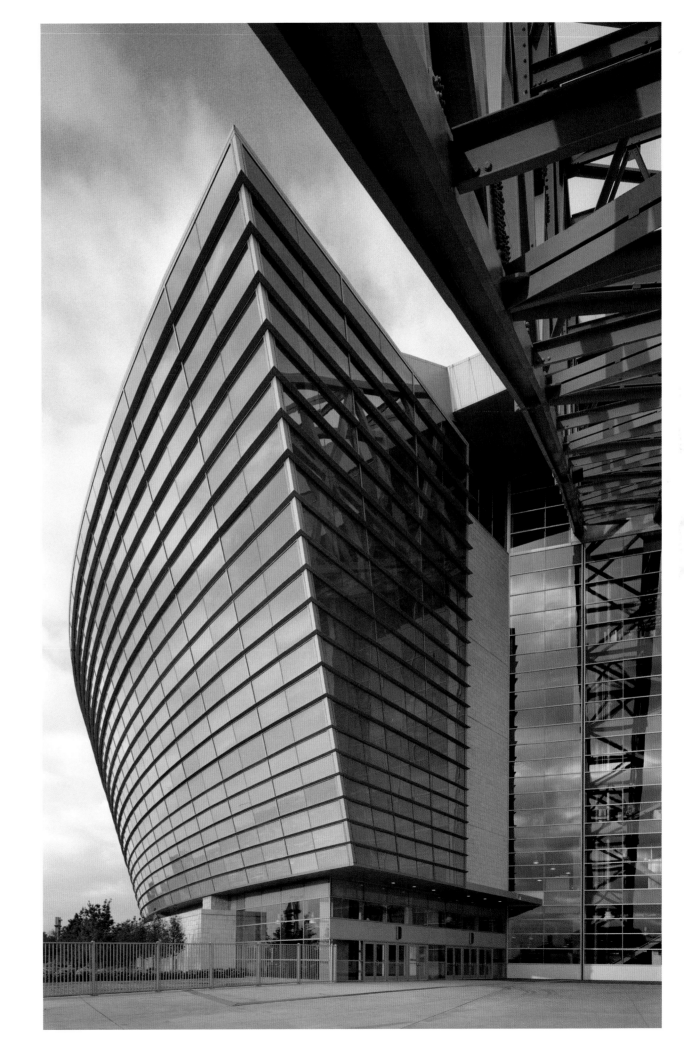

RIGHT The steel arch pierces the glass high above the end-zone door panels.

Everyone was expecting huge pictures of Dallas Cowboys players every-where, but this is a contemporary building and we wanted the art to reflect that, and to be for the average fan, not just the experts.

GENE JONES

OPPOSITE The lead-free glass at the VIP entries provides a crystal-clear glimpse into the heart of the stadium.

Jim Isermann's undulating wall relief offers a mesmerizing counterpoint to the rigidity of nearby pedestrian ramps, while Terry Haggerty's painting *Two Minds* floats above the main concourse. Other significant works—paintings, photography, and works on paper—have been placed in lobbies and corridors, turning the entire building into a lively art walk.

Art was a basic element of the stadium's design from the beginning, an ally and collaborator, playing with or against the architecture but never superficially. Thirteen of the 23 pieces were commissioned for specific spaces; all were chosen by an art council that included Gene Jones, her daughter, Charlotte, and Mary Zlot—a San Francisco art advisor—as well as distinguished curators and collectors from Dallas and Fort Worth. Zlot says the art council provided the "gravitas" they needed to recruit top artists.

Any doubts disappeared the minute the artists saw the spaces they'd be working in: large, highly visible areas where, on a single Sunday afternoon, more people would see their work than in any gallery or museum.

"Everyone was expecting huge pictures of Dallas Cowboys players everywhere," Gene laughs, "but this is a contemporary building and we wanted the

LEFT The ceiling design in the main entry lobby was inspired by a Cartier compact found on Gene Jones's dressing table.

BELOW All 12 public elevators feature images of Cowboys greats, including Michael Irvin.

art to reflect that, and to be for the average fan, not just experts. We put some of the best pieces in the end zones."

Art in sports stadiums is an ancient tradition going back to the Greeks and Romans. The Colosseum and the Circus Maximus were adorned with sculptures, banners, frescoes, and friezes as complements to games and festivals. The Colosseum even had a temporary canvas roof, though no hole in the center, as best we can tell. The art reflected speed, strength, grace, and endurance, qualities that football at its best embodies.

"Jerry understood that art museums are our cathedrals, places where people congregate," says Mary Zlot. "And he could also see how art could enhance what he was trying to do in the stadium."

More Bang for the Buck

Cowboys Stadium also represents a fundamental rethinking of football real estate. In the Roman Colosseum, seating was arranged in concentric rings, connected by concourses and vomitoria. If more seats were needed, another ring was stacked on top.

Most modern sports stadiums, including Texas Stadium, follow this plan, with concourses circling the

bowl like racetracks and bands of suites slipped in between like the rich, creamy center of a layer cake. HKS changed this configuration in the new stadium by clustering most suites and club seats between the goal lines, where most fans want to sit, and then arranging them vertically, like the floors of an office building, instead of stretching them out around the backs of the end zones. Not only are sideline seats more profitable, many fans are willing to exchange end-zone seats for them, even if it means sitting higher up.

The Cowboys also added 52 "dugout" suites at field level, which were the first to sell out despite partially obstructed views. "You can see and hear the players and coaches talking to each other," says Jerry. "It's like having a tailgate party on the 40-yard line."

This arrangement also freed the end-zone platforms, the cheapest real estate in the building, for up to 20,000 standees as well as major corporate sponsors, who are willing to pay extra for all the exposure to network television cameras and the cheering throngs below. Bryan Trubey calls it "the most radical design innovation of all."

LEFT Exposed structure with custom backlit ceiling elements sets the tone for the main concourse clubs.

MIDDLE In the Miller Lite Club, light and sound are catalysts for the players' entry onto the field.

RIGHT Volume and light, combined with strong architectural forms, create an energetic environment in the American Airlines Lounge.

ABOVE The dramatic interplay of
architectural forms creates a sophisticated
backdrop for the Owners Club.

LEFT The historic Ring of Honor incorporates the same letters and numbers from the walls of Texas Stadium and is bracketed by two LED ribbon boards.

Even visitors who are clueless about art and architecture seem to understand that Cowboys Stadium is a special kind of sports palace.

DAVID DILLON

An End and a Beginning

On April 10, 2010, a cool, cloudless Sunday that would have been perfect for football, Texas Stadium came tumbling down. Four million pounds of concrete and two million pounds of steel thundered to earth in a swirl of dust and smoke. The implosion cost the city of Irving $6 million, roughly one-sixth of what Clint Murchison Jr. paid to build the stadium in the first place. It was witnessed by 20,000 spectators who paid $25 per car for the privilege, and tens of thousands more on television and online, some of whom organized special demolition breakfasts to commemorate the moment.

In anticipation of the end, there were emotional recollections of the five Super Bowl championship teams that had called the stadium home; of "Bullet Bob" Hayes, Randy White, and "Roger the Dodger" Staubach, all of whom helped put Dallas on the international sports map for the first time; and of the hardships willingly endured on behalf of "America's Team": ice storms, sunburn, eternal traffic jams, and lost automobiles. The Cowboys were a long love affair, and no sacrifice was too great to see them play.

In these and other ways, Texas Stadium was a product of its time, when pro football still trailed baseball in popularity and no one could conceive of $5 million

wide receivers and $40 million video boards the size of a 747. Its demolition marked the end of an era just as clearly as the opening of Cowboys Stadium marked the beginning of one.

Cowboys Stadium is no longer just a one-season, one-dimensional attraction, pulsating in the fall, dark and gloomy the rest of the year. The end of football season is now more like a short break in the action, before U2, bull riders, and the monster trucks come to town. And even when nothing is happening, school groups and golden agers and the idly curious line up to walk around the stadium—an average of 10,000 a week, half a million a year, more than visited Texas Stadium when it was the second-most popular tourist attraction in Texas after the Alamo.

Even visitors who are clueless about art and architecture seem to understand that Cowboys Stadium is a special kind of sports palace, of its time yet ahead of it as well, a place that transcends the clichés and the tired conventions of professional sports by surrounding them with art, architecture, and the latest technology. Ultimately, everyone involved decided to take a chance on what was new, edgy, and innovative, to roll the dice—and it paid off.

ABOVE Terry Haggerty's *Two Minds* floats above the main concourse.

RIGHT The monumental staircase in the southwest corner of the stadium is surrounded by the artworks of Lawrence Weiner and Franz Ackermann.

LEFT Fans using the pedestrian ramp in the northwest corner of the stadium enjoy the dazzling reflections from Jim Isermann's wall sculpture.

ARTFULLY DONE

CONTEMPORARY EXPRESSIONS ON A MONUMENTAL SCALE

By David Pagel

The new Cowboys Stadium began as a dream: to change the way fans watch football games by making every aspect of the experience more thrilling, gracious, and awe-inspiring than ever before. What takes place on the field is still the focus of any given Sunday. But everything around it has been reinvented, from the groundbreaking architecture of the streamlined structure that has become an instant landmark to the luxurious lounges that make fans feel as if they are in the lobby of a five-star hotel. The same goes for the state-of-the-art digital media board, suspended from the ceiling over the center of the field, which brings the action closer to more fans, making details that flash by in the blink of an eye larger-than-life and even more spectacular.

You do not need to be an art or architecture expert to see that the new Cowboys Stadium is a work of art. From a distance, it looks like an abstract sculpture—its sleek shape and polished surfaces recalling objects often seen in modern museums. From up close, its size and design make an even more powerful impression. And from the moment you step inside the elegant structure, it is clear that you are in for an experience unlike any other. The excitement of watching the game and the thrill of being part of a crowd of as many as 100,000 is matched by the sense that the whole thing has been built with the individual in mind—to make every single visitor's experience unique, satisfying, and unforgettable. Serving up such one-of-a-kind experiences has been one of art's goals from the beginning of time, when cavemen painted pictures on the walls of their caves.

What the Joneses have done is envision the design and oversee the construction of an original building that allows for great intimacy and general civility amid vast crowds of people. That is no small feat. Ordinarily, being in a crowd means being anonymous and faceless, both indistinguishable from everyone else and, in terms of pure numbers, pretty insignificant. Crowds did not become a central feature of human experience until the Industrial Revolution, when factories replaced farms as the dominant way work was organized. Cities formed, concentrating vast numbers of people in urban centers, where they had more spare time than before. Today, most folks go out of their way to avoid crowds, merely tolerating them when it is impossible to avoid them. Most individuals seek the most meaningful experiences of their lives apart from crowds, in more intimate settings—among family and friends, in smaller, more humanly scaled situations.

What is amazing about the new Cowboys Stadium is that its gigantic size does not prevent anyone from feeling as if he or she is being treated as a unique individual, as a valuable visitor whose needs matter and whose desires are important. The architecture of the stadium does this by fusing interior and exterior spaces, where experiences often thought of as being exclusively public or wholly private unfold alongside one another. As a building, the stadium is neither private, like a home, nor public, like a park, street, or freeway. It is an intriguing hybrid, a meeting point between the individual and the group, a location that is both social and sophisticated, open to unpredictable interactions and bounded by the expectations of civil society. In a sense, it is the contemporary equivalent of a fantastic lobby from a nineteenth-

OPPOSITE
Franz Ackermann
Coming Home, 2009
Acrylic on wall
Located in Southwest
Monumental Staircase

ABOVE An Ackermann assistant
carefully maps the brightly colored
landscape.

century European hotel, like the type found in the novels of Thomas Mann. To be in any of its luxurious lounges or stylishly designed shared spaces is to feel as if you are the guest of an especially hospitable establishment, where other guests, who are perfect strangers, also take a break from the rigors of travel and their regular lives, outside the privacy of their rooms and in a space shared by others. Many parts of the stadium have the scale and demeanor of interiors. The elegant architecture, sophisticated décor, and tasteful ornamentation—not to mention the first-rate service and menus—make it easy to forget that one is in a stadium, especially if you are used to run-of-the-mill sports facilities.

It can be more than a little startling—almost disorienting to first-time visitors—to look down to the field and see a game in full swing. The comforts we usually associate with exceptionally well-appointed interiors collide with the size of the structure and what we usually expect from such entities. The best of both worlds comes together in Cowboys Stadium: the pleasurable familiarity of human-scale intimacy and the grandeur and expansiveness of the sheer number of individuals who gather under one big (retractable) roof. It is unlike anything else out there.

An essential feature of this experience and one of the stadium's most exciting innovations is its world-class collection of contemporary art. The 23 works that cover some of the walls of Cowboys Stadium transform the bland passageways of standard-issue stadiums into vital public places—lively locations where people from all walks of life commingle, just as our ancestors have done throughout history in city centers, town squares, busy markets, and bustling plazas. Putting an art collection in a stadium is anything but business as usual. It reflects some profoundly innovative thinking and suggests a very sophisticated notion of what it means to be drawn to the best our culture has to offer.

The Joneses knew that they wanted art in the stadium, and they also knew that this was not their area of expertise. In May 2008 they hired Mary Zlot & Associates, a San Francisco art advisory firm, and invited distinguished leaders of the North Texas cultural community to form an art council that would serve in an advisory capacity to the Jones family in developing an art program. This decision was a smart one. It instantly transformed the old-fashioned relationship between client and consultant into a collaboration among a diverse group of respected experts, each with their own tastes, interests, and convictions and, most importantly, their long-standing commitments to the North Texas cultural community they serve, inhabit, and continue to be a part of. Rather than follow the standard format of an experienced outsider providing advice to a new collector, Zlot quickly created the structure of a group discussion—a lively, flexible forum that took into account the specificity of the context, while making plenty of room for various perspectives, desires, and needs. Michael Auping, chief curator

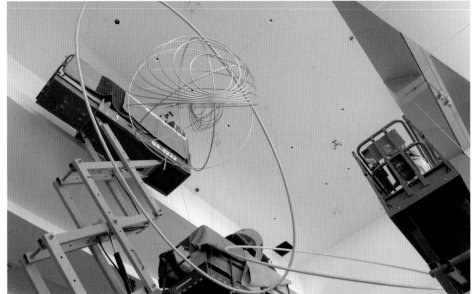

of the Modern Art Museum of Fort Worth; Charlie Wylie, Lupe Murchison curator of contemporary art at the Dallas Museum of Art; Gayle Stoffel and Howard Rachofsky, highly respected collectors of contemporary art; and Melissa Meeks, Director for Two by Two for AIDS and Art, all eagerly agreed to be members of the art council, along with Gene Jones and her daughter, Charlotte Anderson.

At meetings, the art council examined images of works by hundreds of contemporary artists from around the world. They studied the artists' biographies and read countless catalogs, magazines, and articles on Web sites. They discussed, debated, and eventually arrived at this selection of museum-quality pieces by nationally and internationally recognized artists from Texas (Trenton Doyle Hancock and Annette Lawrence); the United States (Ricci Albenda, Doug Aitken, Mel Bochner, Teresita Fernández, Wayne Gonzales, Jacqueline Humphries, Jim Isermann, Dave Muller, Matthew Ritchie, Gary Simmons, Lawrence Weiner, and Garth Weiser); Denmark (Olafur Eliasson); England (Terry Haggerty); France (Daniel Buren); Germany (Franz Ackermann); and Ireland (Eva Rothschild). The art council sought a wide range of works, both in terms of the artists who made them and the styles and media in which they were made. The installations consist of sculptures, paintings, and photographs. Thirteen of its 23 pieces were specially commissioned for the stadium. Eight were chosen from existing bodies of work. Of these, some were

created by American artists who began exhibiting in the 1960s and whose accomplishments are now firmly established parts of art history. Others are by younger artists from Europe and the United States, whose promising careers are just beginning. And still others are by artists who come somewhere between these stages, accomplished mid-career artists whose influence is still growing. The Joneses also commissioned Todd Eberle to photograph the stadium and its collection, which includes his images.

The art collection in the stadium reflects the intimacy of a personal vision. All of its works are multilayered, richly nuanced, physically resplendent, and, most importantly, open to a wide range of interpretations. All invite, sustain, and reward second, third, and fourth looks. None gives away its meanings on first glance. No theme, topic, subject, or style links any one to another, and certainly not all are a homogeneous group. All invite visitors to imaginatively engage them, and to participate actively in the creation of the meanings they generate. All are based in the belief that it is not art's job to tell viewers what to think—or to give simple answers to complex questions—but, instead, to stimulate thinking by getting us to pay attention to details we might otherwise overlook. Generosity, accessibility, and unpretentiousness characterize the collection, which puts a priority on freethinking independence. The Joneses' vision is built on a willingness to take risks. Their collection reflects a commitment to getting the best of everything (and from everyone), and,

most importantly, trusting fans (of art and sport) to come to their own understanding of the family's enterprise.

The works in the collection fall into four groups.

I. Pictures of Places

Doug Aitken, Wayne Gonzales, Trenton Doyle Hancock, Dave Muller, and Gary Simmons make pictures of places. In their art, recognizable things from the world around us become points of departure for imaginative journeys that go every which way.

Initially, Doug Aitken's two pieces, *star* (2008) and *new horizon* (2009), appear to be realistic. Both photographic transparencies are bird's-eye views of cities at night; the first mounted on a light box that spells the word "star" and the second affixed to a light box that is shaped like a star. But closer inspection reveals that Aitken, a Los Angeles artist and filmmaker, has digitally enhanced both photographs, brightening and multiplying the shining streetlights in *star* and turning *new horizon* into a mirror image of itself, its left and right halves exactly matching each other— and glowing like never before. Realism meets artifice in both works, which also invite viewers to step back and read the word "star" or to see the perfect symmetry of its silhouetted shape. Dreamy fantasy comes down to earth in Aitken's crisp pictures of anonymous cities, where everyday reality gives way to multiple layers of meaning, each a little more wondrous for being so close to one another.

Wayne Gonzales has used a similar tactic to make *Cheering Crowd* (2007), a mural-size canvas in various shades of gray and blue that depicts exactly what its title says. The standing crowd of cheering fans looks like crowds everywhere. But something is amiss. To look closely is to see that the New York artist has painted the same seven-foot-square picture three times and hung them side by side. The result is a handmade painting that captures the rhythms of the digital age, when the overwhelming abundance of instantly transmitted images make us both closer and farther apart from one another.

Trenton Doyle Hancock's *From a Legend to a Choir* (2009) presents a different sort of crowd. Set amid a dense garden of cartoon flowers and bright banners emblazoned with the names of crayon colors, Hancock's phantasmagorical figures form a rogues' gallery of misfits: animal-plant hybrids that sometimes look human and at others appear to be black-and-white-striped lumps. The Houston-based artist calls them "mounds," and they are the protagonists in the homemade epic he has been telling for more than a decade, drawing viewers into the freewheeling tale by filling it with all the comedy and tragedy and absurdity of life.

Dave Muller's *Solar Arrangement* (2009) takes a similar big-picture view of life on Earth, pulling back, even farther, to locate our place in the cosmos. In the Los Angeles artist's hand-painted diagram of the solar system, a yellow rose stands in for the sun. Mercury,

ABOVE Mel Bochner's carefully drawn text is charged through punctuation and font.

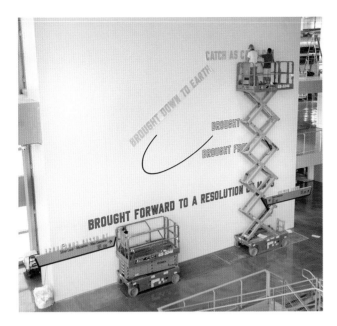

Venus, and Earth are represented by balls of leaves, popcorn, and clover. The yellow rose also recalls the legendary Texas song and hints at Muller's love of music—his life as a trumpet player, DJ, and record collector. Intimate and expansive, Muller's whimsical mural does double-duty as a poetic self-portrait.

Gary Simmons also uses simple images to set up stories that call the imagination into action. *Blue Field Explosions* (2009) is a gigantic cartoon—or an industrial-strength comic book illustration—that not only depicts a pair of powerful explosions but also captures their astonishing energy. To make the huge drawing, the New York artist drew with white oil-stick crayons directly on the wall of the stadium, which had been painted deep blue. Simmons then used his hands to smear the lines, creating the illusion of movement and putting viewers in mind of how swiftly time passes.

II. Moving Through Spaces

The works by Franz Ackermann, Eva Rothschild, Olafur Eliasson, Annette Lawrence, and Jacqueline Humphries require viewers to move around them. Rather than reveal their secrets in an instant—and from one perspective—they seek to move one's emotions by first moving one's feet.

Franz Ackermann's two enormous murals extend over three levels of the stadium and wrap around several walls. It is hard to say where *Coming Home* (2009) ends and *(Meet me) At the Waterfall* (2009)

begins, but what is clear is that the Berlin-based artist has created a lively environment that is a pleasure—and a puzzle—to behold. Its bright colors and funky shapes are based on Ackermann's recollections of several visits to North Texas. More importantly, they invite viewers to take trips, in their imaginations, through the past and into the future—to places that no longer exist and perhaps never will, but can always be visited via art's capacity for imaginative transport.

Eva Rothschild finds mystery in the simplest of things. The components of *Diamonoid* (2009) could not be less poetic: basic geometry (rectangles), basic industrial materials (aluminum and Plexiglas), and basic palette (nothing but jet black). But the way the Dublin-born, London-based artist has composed these unemotional elements is pure magic. Looking into the reflective center of her elegant wall relief from various angles creates the impression of peering into a deep, dark well, where absolute blackness opens into the void and the rational mind comes face to face with things it cannot comprehend.

Olafur Eliasson's pair of sculptural installations likewise puts visitors in mind of infinity. In the southwest entry to the main concourse, *Moving stars takes time* (2008) floats overhead, its six circular components recalling a sleek model of the solar system. But the positions of Eliasson's mirrored glass discs and stainless steel rings do not match those of the planets or any actual constellations. Instead, they

LEFT Dave Muller carefully mixes paint colors for *Solar Arrangement*, an installation that alludes to the solar system.

invite speculation about worlds that exist only in the imagination. Likewise, *Fat super star* (2008–09) draws visitors into its orbit. Hanging in the smaller, more intimate entryway to the Owners Club, the mesmerizing sculpture also functions as a light fixture. Its faceted forms, beautifully crafted from brightly colored glass, mirrors, brass, and halogen bulbs, cast drifting, kaleidoscopic patterns of softly tinted colors on the walls, floor, and ceiling, as well as upon everyone who passes through the foyer. Together, the Copenhagen-born, Berlin-based artist's quiet pieces enliven the spaces around them by making room for wonder, enchantment, and, in the right frame of mind, awe.

Annette Lawrence's *Coin Toss* (2009) springs to life when visitors walk under it. Suspended high overhead in an entrance to the main concourse, the North Texas artist's 45-foot-long sculpture seems to spiral around an invisible axis as a visitor approaches, passes under, and moves on. What actually happens is that dozens of reflected highlights dance along the piece's polished steel cables. Taut as tightropes, the woven cables do not move an inch. But the reflections spiral swiftly, in the same way that a coin spins through space at the start of a game, when the outcome is up in the air, charged with anticipation.

Reflective surfaces also animate Jacqueline Humphries's abstract painting. *Blondnoir* (2008) appears to be two or three paintings that have been shredded and put back together. The New York artist cultivates this effect by painting in layers—by taping off some parts before applying more paint and tearing off the tape. The metallic pigment she uses makes it even more difficult for a viewer to take

ABOVE Matthew Ritchie incorporates vinyl, acrylic, and powder-coated aluminum in creating *Line of Play*.

in everything on first glance. To see Humphries's fractured composition, one must look from various angles, where it never appears to be the same and always discloses more than before.

III. Sign Language

Mel Bochner, Lawrence Weiner, Daniel Buren, Matthew Ritchie, and Garth Weiser use simple words, basic marks, and abstract emblems to create complex experiences. Playing games with language and other types of signs, they make works that are both accessible and ambiguous—as easy to get involved with as they are difficult to stop thinking about.

Mel Bochner's *Win!* (2009) is part of his ongoing "Thesaurus Paintings" series. The New York artist's billboard-size message begins by spelling out its title in plainly printed caps: "WIN!" A series of synonyms follow, complicating the seemingly straightforward title by taking its meaning to extremes. The language gets even more colorful as the words become phrases, each more loaded than the last. The momentum picks up until so many emotions come into play that the original statement fades into the background and language takes on a life of its own, catching everyone in the whirlwind.

Lawrence Weiner plays it cool, using neutral language to paint pictures in the mind's eye of each visitor. The phrases neatly printed on the three-story-tall wall in *BROUGHT UP TO SPEED* (2009) are perfectly

ordinary and capable of describing all sorts of situations. That's where viewers—or readers—come into the conversation set up by the New York artist's multipurpose words. In Weiner's understated, anti-authoritarian, and deeply democratic art, the writing on the wall does not foretell the future so much as it gives visitors the freedom to interpret it in many ways, according to our own interests and desires.

Like Bochner and Weiner, Daniel Buren began his distinguished career in the 1960s, when many avant-garde artists turned away from painting and toward more analytical ways of engaging viewers. Where Bochner and Weiner turned to language, the Frenchman Buren turned to a pattern of 8.5-millimeter-wide stripes. In *Unexpected Variable Configurations: A Work in Situ* (1998), 50 aluminum panels, each printed with Buren's signature stripes in black and white, hang on an immense grid of bright yellow squares. The panels' positions are determined by chance. Not even Buren knows how his piece will look until it is installed. The uncertainty keeps his art fresh and invites viewers to see it—and its surroundings—with fresh eyes.

Matthew Ritchie brings some of the whimsical indeterminacy of gestural painting into the present by using a computer to transform handmade drawings into elaborate plans for mural-scale works that sprawl—like some kind of art virus—across the walls, floors, and ceilings of the spaces where they

are installed. *Line of Play* (2009) is a fragmented triptych that demonstrates how messages change as they are transmitted. Paying homage to such first-generation Conceptual artists as Bochner, Weiner, and Buren, Ritchie treats art as an ongoing experiment that is capable of engaging everything around it—and whatever might lie beyond.

Garth Weiser treats painting as a language: a system of signs that enables communication among the people who use it. *TV Keith* (2008) resembles a corporate logo from which the identifying features have been eliminated. But the black, white, and gray abstraction is also a concise survey of various ways artists apply paint: fluidly, with brushes; atmospherically, with spray guns; and thickly, with palette knives. With great efficiency, the New York painter packs ample punch into his nearly symmetrical image, suggesting that the language of painting is resilient and enduring.

IV. User-Friendly Abstraction

Ricci Albenda, Terry Haggerty, Jim Isermann, and Teresita Fernández transform abstraction into a user-friendly enterprise that is optimistic, engaging, and individualistic. Their commissioned works address visitors as individuals who are part of crowd, unique people who make up an inconceivably large group.

Ricci Albenda's *Interior Landscape, Full Spectrum* (2009) deconstructs the rainbow, turning its

graceful curves and gently mixed bands of color into sharp, geometric forms and crisp, unmixed tints. Altering the rainbow may sound like a no-win proposition, but the New York artist's 130-foot-long painting—or series of nearly two-dozen oddly shaped monochromes—never pretends to beat Nature at its own game. More digital than organic, Albenda's abstraction brings some of the wonder of the outside world into an architectural setting with its own style and substance.

Terry Haggerty's similarly sized stripe painting, *Two Minds* (2009), also invites double takes. Its hand-painted bands of candy-cane red and white appear to be continuous and consistent—like the stripes of a gigantic banner gently flapping in the wind. But to look closely is to see that what initially appeared to be realistic is an illusion: there is no way the left and right halves of the London-born, Berlin-based artist's image hold together. This deliberate glitch gives the painting its kick and explains its title. What we know and what we see are different, and the only way to account for both is to be of two minds.

Jim Isermann's monumental wall relief combines the logic of industrial production with the freedom of art, forming an indescribable hybrid that is a pleasure to see. The components of Isermann's *Untitled* (2009–10) are unbelievably simple: straight lines and white triangles. But what the Wisconsin-born, Palm Springs-based artist does with them defies

explanation. His faceted abstraction makes the wall come alive—to appear to swell and recede, as if it were breathing. Sunlight enhances the effect. As it moves across the undulating composition, highlights and shadows skip and leap in a rhythmic dance that is both sensible and marvelous.

Teresita Fernández's *Starfield* (2009) reminds visitors of the vastness of the cosmos and our humble place in it. On a shiny black wall, the Cuba-born, New York-based artist has affixed a constellation of glass blocks, each the size of an ice cube and each with a mirrored back. From up close, visitors see themselves in the tiny mirrors. From farther back, ghostly silhouettes appear in the glossy blackness. *Starfield* suffuses the space between things with a sensual charge that transforms otherwise incidental details into evocations of infinity.

To record the unique beauty of the art in the stadium, and to document the stadium itself, the Jones family enlisted New York-based artist-photographer Todd Eberle. His stunning photographs invite people to see their surroundings more clearly than usual. Sometimes Eberle steps back and takes in a big-picture view, capturing the sweep and the scope of a setting by making its architecture the star of the show. At others, he focuses on details, zooming in to reveal the beauty of abstract patterns, the simplicity of geometric forms, and the gracefulness of spaces carved out by modern buildings. Eberle often presents his photographs in pairs, creating charged

juxtapositions that bring the imagination into the picture and make us see unexpected connections. His paired pictures change the way we perceive the world by enriching our understanding of places and what takes place in them.

All of the artists whose works are in this collection have pieces in the permanent collections of prestigious museums across the country. Many have similar pieces in museums all over the world. Their works in the stadium would not be out of place in any of those institutions. Few museums, however, have enough space to permanently exhibit works as large as many of the ones here. Trenton Doyle Hancock's *From a Legend to a Choir* and Jim Isermann's *Untitled* sculptural relief each measure more than 40 feet tall by 100 feet long. Franz Ackermann's two murals cover nearly as much area, wrapping around two walls on three levels of the stadium. Paintings and installations by Ricci Albenda, Daniel Buren, Terry Haggerty, and Dave Muller each measure approximately 21 by 125 feet. And other sculptures and wall works, by Mel Bochner, Olafur Eliasson, Annette Lawrence, Matthew Ritchie, Gary Simmons, and Lawrence Weiner, range from 40 to 70 feet on a side.

Unlike most private collections, which hang in homes or in the halls of large corporations, this one is accessible to crowds that can exceed 100,000 in a single day. It is there to be seen, week after week, season after season, by tourists just passing through

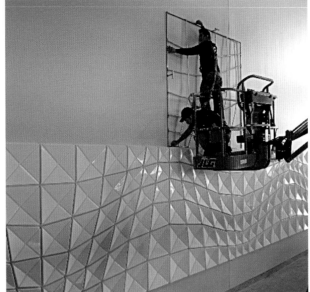

and by regulars, who, in returning again and again, grow familiar with the works they are fond of, develop favorites, and maybe even change their minds about others.

The art in the stadium is more integrated into the hustle and bustle of modern life than it would be if it were in a museum. It appears in unexpected places—overhead in grand entries, around the corners in wide stairways, and along the walls of huge ramps. Visitors who think that art needs the quiet privacy of guarded galleries are in for a surprise. It looks great in the stadium. It holds its own amid the crowds. And it transforms massive public spaces into one-of-a-kind meeting places—impossible-to-mistake locations where visitors from all over the world come together to share the experience.

Sports and art are not typically thought of as belonging together. In fact, most Americans simply presume that the two activities have so little in common that they are at opposite ends of the spectrum: sports belonging to the athletically inclined and art being the province of the aesthetically inclined. In other words, mind or body, brains or brawn, refined or raw. But in the Joneses' vision, great sporting events and great works of art do something similar: they get people talking.

When it comes to sports, fans talk about games with great passion, discussing the relative merits of owners' decisions, coaches' strategies, referees' calls, and

players' performances. Current games and recent seasons are compared and contrasted to those from the past, creating a living history in which fact and fiction are interwoven so that legends sometimes grow to mythical proportions.

When it comes to art, everyone is a critic. Viewers talk about art with the same passion that fans bring to football—discussing, debating, assessing, analyzing, and arguing over high points and low, new artists and old, accomplishments and missteps, game-changing innovations and replays of old favorites.

Ultimately, the point of both sports and art is that they make the people who gather around them just a little bit more civilized. At their best, sports and art bring together people from all walks of life to savor and delight in those things we cherish. For fans of both, sports and art are voluntary activities, otherwise unnecessary entertainments that are more than diversions because they stir our deepest beliefs by exciting us to share them with others—to define ourselves, as individuals and as groups, by articulating in public what we value in private. Nowhere else in the country is this more graciously facilitated than at the new Cowboys Stadium, where art and sports work in concert to enhance every fan's visit.

OLAFUR ELIASSON
MOVING STARS TAKES TIME (2008)

Stainless steel, polished stainless steel, glass mirror, color-effect filter glass,
color foil, powder-coated steel, steel cable
Approximate dimensions spanning: 25 feet by 45 feet by 20 feet
Site-specific commission
LOCATED IN MAIN CONCOURSE CLUB, ENTRY F

The rapid pace of modern life is often driven by the sense that we need to know what is going on in the blink of an eye—or, at the very least, well before it is yesterday's news.

Olafur Eliasson's *Moving stars takes time* (2008) goes out of its way to frustrate this desire. As a sculpture, it looks incomplete, more like a finely designed and beautifully polished model of some of the planets and moons in our solar system than a typical mobile, whose elements would counterbalance one another in a more resolved fashion. It is also different from conventional sculptures because its six components refuse to command the space they occupy with the authority common to more massive works. And Eliasson's quiet piece avoids the flashy razzle-dazzle of some contemporary art, which makes a spectacle of itself to grab headlines.

None of this is accidental. Eliasson's purpose in making *Moving stars takes time* is to get viewers to slow down for a moment, to take a brief break from the relentless rush of modern life and stop behaving as if it is absolutely essential that we know what something means the split second we see it. Such thinking makes sense on the highway, when we need to know the speeds of oncoming traffic because our survival depends on it. But it is unsuitable for more nuanced activities, like understanding the complexities of science, comprehending the beauty of art, and savoring the ambiguity of both. Being comfortable with uncertainty is the first step in a process that requires viewer participation and leads to thinking outside the box. Eliasson's art calls us to contemplate our place in the universe, where there is plenty of room for mystery, for wonder, and for much, much more than we can understand.

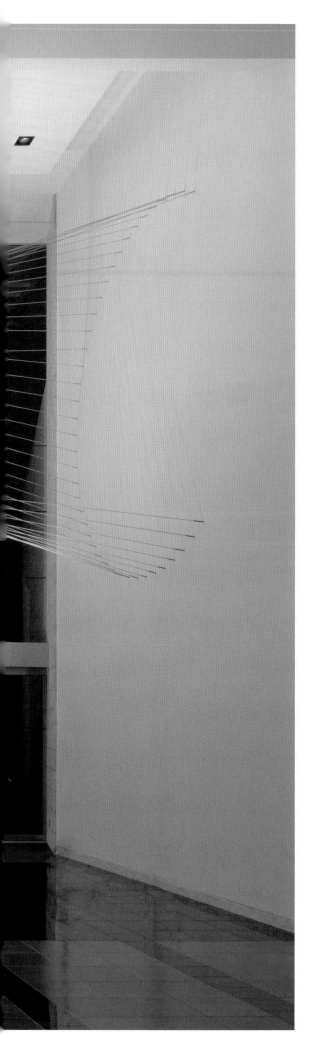

ANNETTE LAWRENCE
COIN TOSS (2009)

Stranded cable
14 feet diameter by approximately 45 feet (span)
Site-specific commission
LOCATED IN MAIN CONCOURSE CLUB, ENTRY E

Just about every sculpture that has ever been made has had to struggle against gravity—to fight against its downward tug, to rise up off the ground, and to stand tall, with the authority of a monument. Mobiles are different because they hang from the ceiling. But their effect also depends upon their capacity to defy gravity—so that they seem to float in midair.

Annette Lawrence's graceful sculpture stands apart from this history for one simple reason: gravity does not matter to it. As an original work of art, it has as much to do with the nearly immaterial installations of California's Light and Space movement as it does with the geometric sculptures of such New York Minimalists as Donald Judd and Fred Sandback. Lawrence's tautly stretched steel cables inhabit an architectural interior, enhancing the grand entrance by giving elegant form to the passage of time and the movement of bodies through space.

The North Texas artist's hourglass-shaped sculpture comes alive when one walks under it. That is when the gentle curves of its profile shift, causing the open volume it wraps around to appear to contract and expand. Dazzling reflections dance off its shiny silver cables. The faster one walks, the faster they spiral through space. This movement is suggested by the work's title: *Coin Toss* (2009) calls to mind the start of each game, when a coin spins through space in a manner very similar to that described by Lawrence's streamlined sculpture, which commands a lot more space than it actually occupies.

MATTHEW RITCHIE
LINE OF PLAY (2009)

Powder-coated aluminum, vinyl, acrylic
East Wall, West Wall: 30 feet by 20 feet
Ceiling: 34 feet by 10 feet
Site-specific commission
LOCATED IN MAIN CONCOURSE CLUB, ENTRY K

Made of powder-coated aluminum, vinyl, and acrylic paint, Matthew Ritchie's *Line of Play* (2009) transforms the age-old medium of drawing. The work becomes a metaphor for the many ways people make sense of just about everything, from our surroundings to life's purpose to whatever might lie beyond. In Ritchie's hands, art is an ongoing experiment—an ever-expanding inquiry we puzzle over as we discover new ideas, change our minds about old ones, and come up with more questions.

It all starts with the marks coaches make when they diagram plays. Ritchie transfers the Xs and Os they draw on chalkboards to a computer, where he turns them into swirling force fields of animated energy. The London-born, New York-based artist describes *Line of Play* as two figures passing something between them. It does not take a great leap to see what he means, even if it is impossible to identify those figures and that object. That is the point. Ritchie's futuristic triptych does not depict things we already know so much as it gives us a glimpse of things we have never seen.

Ritchie emerged as an artist in the 1990s, when the Information Age entered into its digital phase and the Internet made more information accessible to more people than ever before. His works are all based on the possibilities presented by technology's capacity to bring together advanced systems of inquiry. Ritchie often collaborates with neurologists, physicists, philosophers, historians, and game theorists in order to push knowledge, consciousness, and beliefs beyond their existing limits.

DOUG AITKEN
STAR (2008)

Neon-lit light box
45 inches by 119 inches by 10 inches
Edition 2 of 4
Acquisition
LOCATED ON HALL OF FAME LEVEL, ENTRY A

Everyone knows the saying "A picture speaks a thousand words." But what about words that are also pictures? Do they say more? Less? Something different? These are some of the questions Doug Aitken's *star* (2008) invites viewers to ponder.

From across the hall, it is easy to read Aitken's ten-foot-long word. But "star" refers to many things, from the heavenly bodies twinkling in the night sky to actors and athletes, who shine for different reasons. "Star" is a noun and a verb, a word that describes people and what they do when they become the focus of our attention.

From up close, language fades into the background as viewers get lost in the details of the picture that creates the word. The Los Angeles artist and filmmaker photographed a city at night and digitally enhanced its shining streetlights so that they call to mind the stars overhead. The dazzling image on his neon light box lets us imagine that we are looking down at the earth's surface from above while simultaneously staring up at the heavens. The illusion is even more wondrous because Aitken created it with a picture of an otherwise unremarkable location—not a famous city with a signature skyline but just an everyday place that could be anywhere.

His fusion of words and pictures builds on art made of language by such influential precedents as Lawrence Weiner, Mel Bochner, and Ed Ruscha. Bringing fantasy into the picture, Aitken melds illusion and reality into an experience of thrilling stillness.

EVA ROTHSCHILD
DIAMONOID (2009)

Powder-coated aluminum, Plexiglas
70 inches by 110 inches by 7 1/2 inches
Edition 1 of 3
Acquisition
LOCATED IN HALL OF FAME LEVEL, ENTRY A

In the 1960s, artists on the West Coast made sculptures whose shimmering finishes were as sleek as custom-painted hot rods. Sculptors on the East Coast stuck to less flashy finishes, preferring subdued colors, industrial ruggedness, and simple geometry—often repeated to form the rows, stacks, and columns of their serial works. Today, Dublin-born and London-based Eva Rothschild combines characteristics of both types of Minimalism. At once seductive and structurally rigorous, her works are as pleasurable to perceive as they are satisfying to contemplate.

From across the room, *Diamonoid* (2009) appears to be a basic black diamond. But as soon as a viewer moves in any direction, the illusion of stillness, flatness, and smooth uniformity disintegrates. Reflections and shadows dance across the mirror-like surface of the specially treated plastic that forms the diamond-shaped backdrop of Rothschild's wall relief. Similar reflections race along the numerous aluminum bars that echo the shape of the nearly ten-foot-long monochrome.

The best visual effects, however, take place between the powder-coated bars and the industrial-strength Plexiglas, where Rothschild makes it difficult for viewers to distinguish between the shifting geometry of the eccentrically angled bars and their crisp reflections in the ink-black plastic. The impression is that of peering into a deep, dark well, where light does not penetrate and tangible reality seems to open into the void. With understated efficiency, Rothschild suggests that this is where the magic—and the mystery—of art begin.

DAVE MULLER
SOLAR ARRANGEMENT (2009)

Acrylic on wall
Approximately 21 feet by 131 feet
Site-specific commission
LOCATED IN MAIN CONCOURSE, NORTHWEST CONCESSION

Like many school kids all over the country, Dave Muller's first visit to a football field had nothing to do with sports. His science teacher took his class to the local stadium to demonstrate just how big the solar system is. Using a Ping-Pong ball for the sun, which was placed on one goal line, they needed the entire field, as well as the stands beyond the opposite end zone, to make their accurately scaled model.

Solar Arrangement (2009) plays off Muller's memory of that experience. In his expansive mural, the sun is represented by a gorgeous yellow rose. The first three planets, Mercury, Venus, and Earth, are represented by a ball of dry leaves, a ball of crunchy popcorn, and a ball of lush clover. Dashed lines trace small sections of their orbits. Several stars, which resemble snowflakes, twinkle in the background. The hand-drawn, hand-painted richness of Muller's image makes it intimate and endearing, far warmer and more enchanting than standard diagrams. Muller's whimsical picture of the innermost part of our solar system also plays off the "You Are Here" notations found on maps and floor plans in such big public places as malls, parks, and stadiums.

Muller invites us to ponder our place in the cosmos—to picture the huge crowd gathered here as a tiny speck beneath the heavens. The experience is humbling and eye-opening, both personal and universal. And like much of Muller's art, *Solar Arrangement* has a musical component. Muller is a Los Angeles artist who is also a trumpet player, DJ, and record collector. His sun evokes "The Yellow Rose of Texas," a legendary song that has been covered again and again and never the same way twice.

TERRY HAGGERTY
TWO MINDS (2009)

Acrylic on wall
Approximately 21 feet by 126 feet
Site-specific commission
LOCATED IN MAIN CONCOURSE, NORTHEAST CONCESSION

As its title, *Two Minds* (2009), suggests, Terry Haggerty's painting is conflicted. On one hand, it presents a system that fuses crisp visual punch with consistent, all-over evenness. On the other, it insists that the quirks provided by unexpected interruptions make art and life both interesting and unpredictable, at once puzzling and fun.

It is impossible to look at Haggerty's mural without your eyes instantly gliding along its wavy bands of color. From one end to the other, we visually travel back and forth along the candy cane-colored curves—up and down, over and under—as if on a roller-coaster ride. Brightly striped awnings come to mind, as do circus tents, banners flapping in the wind, garments in Baroque paintings, and 1960s Op Art.

Haggerty's painting creates the illusion of three-dimensional space by suggesting that some sections recede into the distance and disappear behind other sections. The mind's eye fills in what is not visible, creating a coherent image. And this is where the London-born, Berlin-based artist throws a monkey wrench into the system.

It is physically impossible for the red and white stripes to curve up and over the "fold" or the "bump" in the upper-middle part of the painting. There is simply no way for the stripes to be continuous, unbroken bands. But that is what the mind's eye wants to see. It's also what our eyes tell us, when carried away by the painting's visual momentum. And that is exactly what Haggerty wants—a glitch in the system that makes room for idiosyncrasy and allows us to be of two minds.

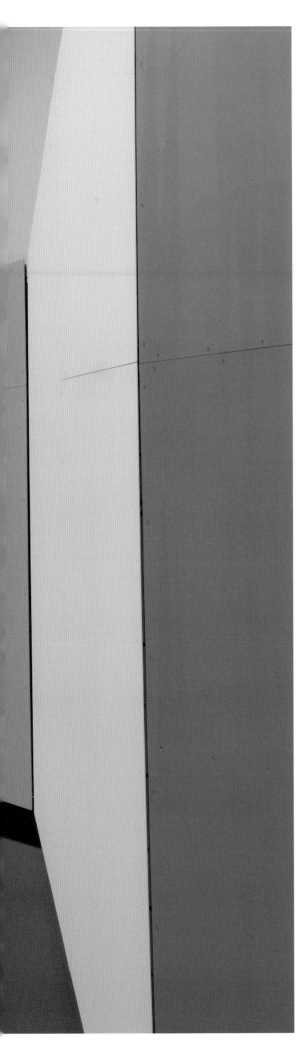

RICCI ALBENDA
INTERIOR LANDSCAPE, FULL SPECTRUM (2009)

Acrylic on aluminum panels
Approximately 21 feet by 131 feet
Site-specific commission
LOCATED IN MAIN CONCOURSE, SOUTHWEST CONCESSION

Ricci Albenda's *Interior Landscape, Full Spectrum* (2009) takes visitors in two directions: back in time to pre-Renaissance Europe, where painting and architecture were intimately related, and into the future, where painting and architecture are again integrated, but this time in the virtual world of digital information. Albenda's visually tricky installation plays up the confusion between two-dimensional illusions and three-dimensional space to make visitors aware of our surroundings and alert to art's power to change them.

This New York artist begins with the architecture on which his 130-foot-long painting—or series of oddly shaped paintings—rests: the gently curved wall that wraps around the field and follows the graceful oval shape of the stadium. Albenda breaks the smooth continuity of the wall into a fractured fun house of color, affixing nearly two dozen aluminum panels to it. Each panel has four sides but none is square, or even rectangular. No two are the same shape, nor does a right angle appear to define any of their corners, which tend toward extremes. As for their colors, no two are the same. Although they cover the spectrum, Albenda has replaced the natural violet, red, and yellow of the rainbow with such tints as lavender, coral, and ochre.

Arranged side by side in an eccentric row, Albenda's beautifully painted panels appear to recede and protrude, as if pulsating like a peculiar, geometric heartbeat. The two-dimensional space of painting and the three-dimensional space of architecture are no longer separate. They come together to trick the eye and delight the mind.

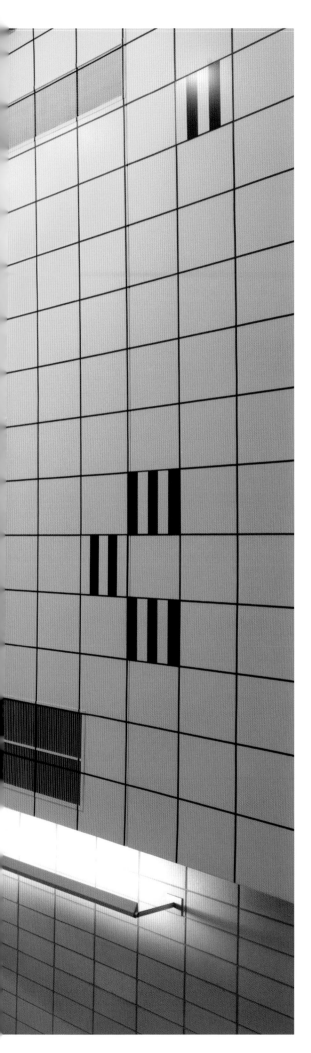

DANIEL BUREN
UNEXPECTED VARIABLE CONFIGURATIONS:
A WORK IN SITU (1998)

Wall painted yellow with hand-drawn grid and
50 screen-printed aluminum plates
Approximately 21 feet by 118 feet
Editions 10 of 15 and 11 of 15
Acquisition
LOCATED IN MAIN CONCOURSE, SOUTHEAST CONCESSION

Daniel Buren's bright yellow wall painting fits into its surroundings at the same time that it stands out from them. This back-and-forth ambiguity leads many viewers to ask: "Is it art or just part of the building?" And that is exactly what the veteran French artist wants you to ask, both of his signature stripe works and everything that has been made by mankind.

Buren's point is that it is too limiting to think of art as only a precious object that needs to be sheltered from daily life and sequestered in a museum. In his radically democratic view, art is most compelling when it is unexpected, especially when it interacts with its context and alters our perceptions by getting us to think more clearly about the world we inhabit.

Buren began his distinguished career in the early 1960s. At that time, messy, abstract painting had become cliché: little more than a painter's trademark or readily marketed brand. Buren's solution was to use ready-made pieces of striped canvas. In 1965, he selected a standard pattern: solid vertical stripes—in red, blue, yellow, green, orange, brown, or black—alternating with white stripes of the same width, 8.5 centimeters. In 1967, Buren took the next step. He abandoned canvas and began printing his now trademark stripes on posters, which he affixed to walls, fences, benches, and phone booths all over Paris.

Unexpected Variable Configurations: A Work in Situ (1998) is classic Buren. On an immense expanse of identical yellow squares hang 50 aluminum panels, each printed with a black-and-white or white-and-black pattern. The positions of the panels are determined by chance. Surprise is built into the system. And like all of Buren's works, this one invites double takes as viewers see art—and everything around it—with fresh eyes.

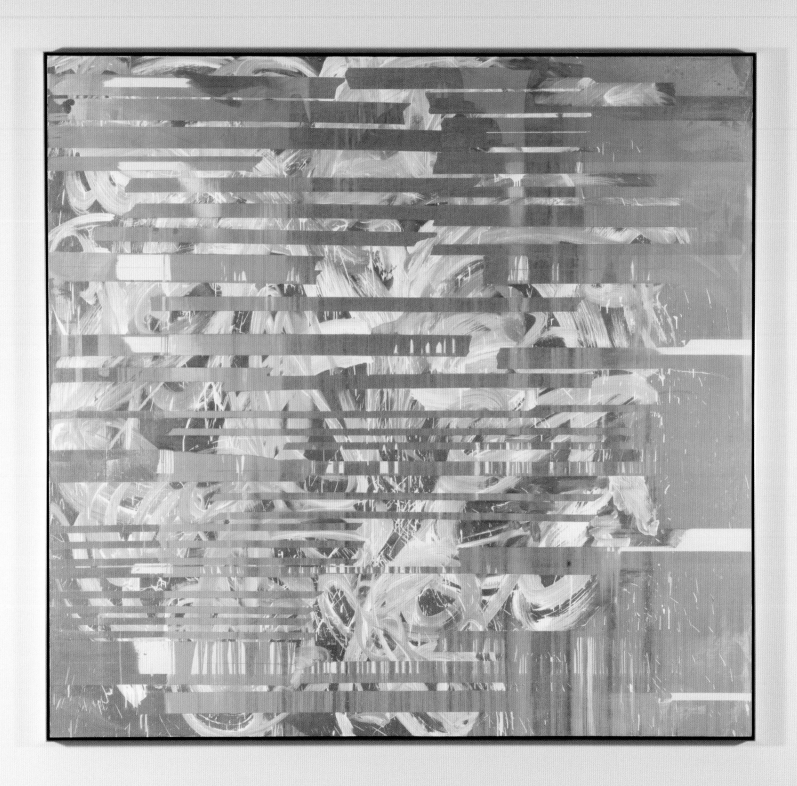

JACQUELINE HUMPHRIES
BLONDNOIR (2008)

Oil and enamel on linen
90 inches by 96 inches
Acquisition
LOCATED ON HALL OF FAME LEVEL, OWNERS CLUB

Jacqueline Humphries's *Blondnoir* (2008) appears to be two or three paintings collapsed into the same space. Think high-speed collision. Or a digital transmission on the fritz. The New York artist's fractured, silver-hued abstraction gives stunning shape to the compression of time and space that makes modern life both thrilling and anxiety riddled.

In the nineteenth century, philosophers felt that the Sublime delivered such double-edged experiences. Humphries, influenced by her predecessors in the New York School of painting, brings these experiences down to earth. The metallic silver paint she mixes herself is highly reflective. Its glare can be blinding. So to see her work without squinting, one must look at it from various angles, from across the room and up close. Taking it in from different perspectives allows the viewer to appreciate its splintered, stop-and-start composition.

Its title, made up of two adjectives Humphries has joined, evokes light and darkness, beauty and menace. And like a movie from the glory days of film noir, her painting requires that viewers do a little detective work, piecing together the evidence to see the light amid the shadows.

To this end, Humphries hides nothing. A close look reveals that *Blondnoir* was painted in layers. Each layer dried before the next was applied. And between layers, Humphries covered parts of her painting with strips of masking tape, sometimes sticking it on in parallel bands and at other times with less regularity. The process—painting, taping, painting again, and tearing off the tape—has created a charged surface of interrupted brushstrokes and fragmented shapes that recalls cut-and-paste collage and roughly spliced films. The drama and the suspense are there for any viewer who is not afraid to play detective.

GARTH WEISER
TV KEITH (2008)

Acrylic and gouache on canvas
93 inches by 83 inches
Acquisition
LOCATED ON HALL OF FAME LEVEL, OWNERS CLUB

Garth Weiser strips painting down to the basics. *TV Keith* (2008) is a large abstract canvas from which color has been almost entirely eliminated. The same goes for the free-form gestures that ordinarily provide evidence of the artist's touch and typically give abstract art its hand-made originality. In the young New York-based painter's no-nonsense canvas, the shapes are common, the lines are precise, and the composition is rudimentary, a nearly symmetrical division of top and bottom, left and right, circles and rectangles.

Despite the reductive format, Weiser's work is anything but limited. This deceptively simple image is equally engaged with the materials and techniques of its construction, the world around it, and the history of Minimalist abstraction. It makes room for fascinating reflections about painting's capacity to multitask, to be not only many things to many people, but to be many things to individual viewers, all at once.

To apply paint, Weiser uses brushes, palette knives, and spray guns. Some parts of his image are atmospheric, others are flat expanses, and still others appear to be three-dimensional, jutting forward like a steely cone, or overlapping like a target's concentric rings. The line that divides the airy top of the painting from its rock-solid bottom recalls the horizon of wide-open spaces and evokes the landscape of Montana, where Weiser was born. The stylized simplicity of corporate logos and the crisp efficiency of graphic design play important roles in Weiser's multilayered work, which also recalls the test patterns and static that often appeared on TV screens in the days before the world went digital.

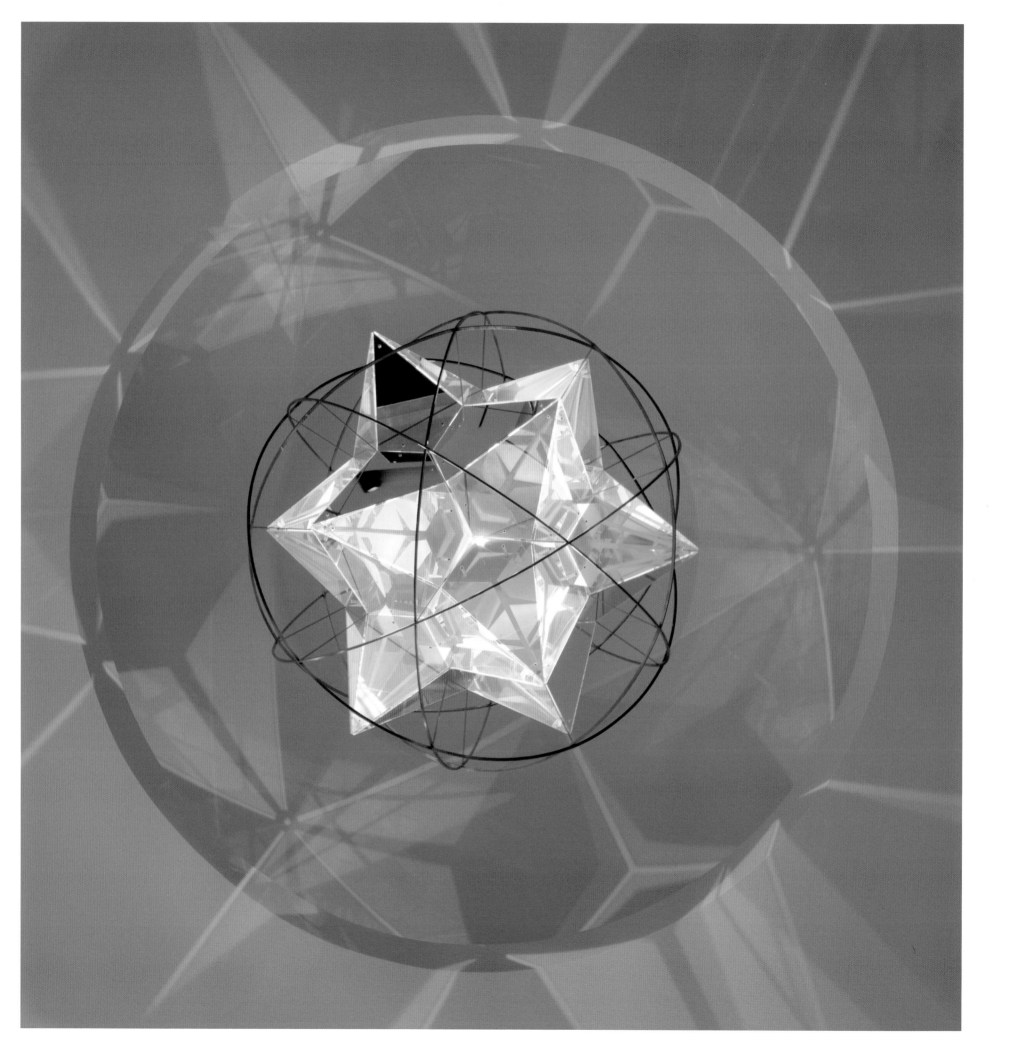

OLAFUR ELIASSON
FAT SUPER STAR (2008-09)

Brass, color-effect filter glass, mirror, halogen light fixture
39 3/8 inches by 39 3/8 inches by 39 3/8 inches
Edition 2 of 10
Acquisition
LOCATED ON HALL OF FAME LEVEL, OWNERS CLUB

Olafur Eliasson's *Fat super star* (2008–09) is one of two pieces that the Danish artist of Icelandic heritage has installed at the stadium. Its partner, *Moving stars takes time* (2008) occupies the southwest entry of the main concourse and consists of six circular components that slowly spin overhead, like an elegant version of an astronomical model of the solar system. *Fat super star* also hangs from the ceiling, but it inhabits a much smaller, more intimate entryway, where it stars in a show all its own.

As is always the case with Eliasson's contemplative art, the show is not an extravagant drama or eye-grabbing spectacle. More like a whisper than a shout, it is a quiet reminder of the beauty of light, the magic of happenstance, and the unforgettable resonance of some of life's most fleeting experiences.

Eliasson's star, wrapped in brass bands that suggest elliptical orbits, recalls holiday decorations, religious symbols, children's toys, and the stars in the sidewalk of Hollywood Boulevard. It also resembles a giant jewel, with gorgeously cut facets reflecting every color of the spectrum. But rather than settling on any one of these interpretations, *Fat super star* evokes a more expansive, even universal, experience. It does not take a great leap of the imagination to see Eliasson's piece as a homemade rainbow. Ingeniously crafted from tinted glass, mirrors, brass, and halogen light fixtures, it casts kaleidoscopic patterns on the domed ceiling and shines soft beams of light on visitors, who become part of the art. Eliasson's star is a focal point that disperses attention around the room, inviting everyone to be attentive to everything—and everyone—present.

JIM ISERMANN
UNTITLED (2009-10)

Vacuum-formed styrene wall
40 feet by 96 feet
Site-specific commission
LOCATED ON NORTHWEST RAMP WALL

Jim Isermann's gigantic wall relief was conceived and fabricated with the individual in mind. Its basic unit is a seven-foot-square module. This building block is slightly larger than an adult, familiar proportions that do not stretch the imagination, overwhelm the senses, or test the limits of comprehension.

That is what Isermann does when he lays out his human-scale building blocks, arranging 65 of them by turning every other one in the opposite direction of its neighbors. This simple gesture creates a complex pattern that transforms a 4,000-square-foot wall into an astonishingly beautiful abstraction that is a marvel of engineering and a pleasure to behold.

For the logically minded, Isermann's work is an abstract jigsaw puzzle to be taken apart and reassembled in the mind's eye. To study any of its seven-foot sections is to see that each consists of 36 smaller panels that come in 11 different designs, making for nearly 2,500 separate parts. For the intuitively inclined, it is not difficult to understand Isermann's

goals by stepping back and taking in an overall view. He makes basic shapes add up to wholly unexpected experiences that defy explanation as they fuse art, design, and architecture.

Isermann was born in Kenosha, Wisconsin, and now lives and works in Palm Springs, California. For the last 30 years, he has been at the forefront of a movement to combine the logic of industrial production with the freedom of art—to unite the clarity of rationality with the thrill of something more. From wherever one stands, Isermann's magnificently user-friendly installation embodies the excitement of being part of something bigger and more profound than usual.

TRENTON DOYLE HANCOCK
FROM A LEGEND TO A CHOIR (2009)

Vinyl print
Approximately 40 feet by 98 feet
Site-specific commission
LOCATED ON SOUTHEAST RAMP WALL

Trenton Doyle Hancock's dense work stops visitors in their tracks. Its screaming colors and riotous energy are an eyeful and not for the fainthearted. But what happens when a viewer spends a few moments with Hancock's crazy quilt of an image is hardly indelicate. *From a Legend to a Choir* (2009) builds upon the most democratic aspects of American Pop Art, from Stuart Davis to Andy Warhol to Jean-Michel Basquiat, empowering viewers by letting us bring our own stories to a wildly open-ended narrative.

Hancock's sprawling mural sets the stage. Its flower-filled setting evokes the biblical Garden of Eden and the psychedelic Summer of Love. Its figures' striped outfits recall jailhouse garb. Hancock's cast of characters is a rogues' gallery: some are headless lumps and others look more like animals than human beings, with a walrus, a four-eyed rooster, and other mutants.

These creatures are part of an ongoing saga that Hancock has been telling for the past decade. He calls them "mounds"—plant-animal hybrids that behave like all of us, sometimes admirably and sometimes badly. Hancock's homegrown mythology includes a creation story, an epic battle between good and evil, an attempt at reconciliation between color-loving carnivores and scrawny, subterranean vegans, and much more. It has its roots in his personal history. Now based in Houston, Hancock was born in Oklahoma City and raised in Paris, Texas. He is the stepson of a preacher. His roots nourish an inventive imagination out of which springs a world so rich with possibility that viewers cannot help but be drawn into it.

DOUG AITKEN
NEW HORIZON (2009)

LED-lit light box
66 inches by 70 inches by 8 1/4 inches
Edition 3 of 4
Acquisition
LOCATED ON HALL OF FAME LEVEL, SOUTHWEST ELEVATOR LOBBY

Doug Aitken's works grab the eye in a split second. Just as quickly, they invite second looks. Then the game is on: what had seemed obvious becomes complex and open to interpretation.

From far away, Aitken's *new horizon* (2009) resembles the shiny blue star on the Cowboys' helmet. The oval glow at its center recalls the glare of bright lights on a glossy curved surface. From up close, however, it is apparent that Aitken's nearly six-foot-tall star is actually a laser-sharp photograph of a city's coastline, shot at night from a plane or helicopter. The Los Angeles artist and filmmaker has mounted his photographic transparency onto an LED light box. This causes the lights depicted in the image to do what they actually do in the real world: illuminate their surroundings. The picture comes alive as it eliminates the difference between doing and showing, function and form.

Aitken has also used a computer to digitally manipulate the image, making its left and right halves into mirror images of each other. Like a high-tech Rorschach ink blot, the perfectly symmetrical image emphasizes the artifice at the heart of Aitken's photographs and films. Many of his movies unfold slowly, some across several screens, not telling stories so much as evoking moods and creating atmospheres. Like them, *new horizon* never lets viewers forget that we are looking at a still image as it draws us into a drama both serene and strange, at once commonplace and extraordinary.

WAYNE GONZALES
CHEERING CROWD (2007)

Acrylic on canvas, triptych
7 feet by 21 feet
Acquisition
LOCATED ON HALL OF FAME LEVEL, SOUTHWEST ELEVATOR LOBBY

The biggest difference between watching a game on TV and going to the real thing is the crowd. There is simply no substitute for being there, immersed in the mass of humanity that has gathered to root for the home team.

The biggest difference between looking at a painting over the Internet and seeing it in person is the detail. There is simply no substitute for being there, face-to-face with paint on canvas.

The various differences between first- and second-hand experience is the subject of Wayne Gonzales's *Cheering Crowd* (2007), a wall-sized canvas in various shades of gray that depicts exactly what its title says. To scan it quickly is to see one big crowd, perhaps a section from a stadium like this one. But as the eye glides across the New York artist's three-panel painting, it picks up rhythms and settles into patterns. Soon, one notices that the 7-by-21-foot picture is actually three seven-foot-square canvases, each of which depicts the very same scene, a photo Gonzales culled from the Internet.

The repetition recalls Andy Warhol's early Pop works, which presented multiple images of tabloid news photos, often of disasters and tragedies. Gonzales brings Warhol's focus on the mechanics of the mass media into the digital age, where the crowds are bigger and the information transmitted much faster. Yet Gonzales makes his paintings slowly, by hand. To view them up close is to see the image disintegrate into an energized field of individual brushstrokes. Simultaneously intimate and anonymous, his art captures the sensation of losing one's self in a crowd only to find yourself as a part of something bigger, more powerful and profound.

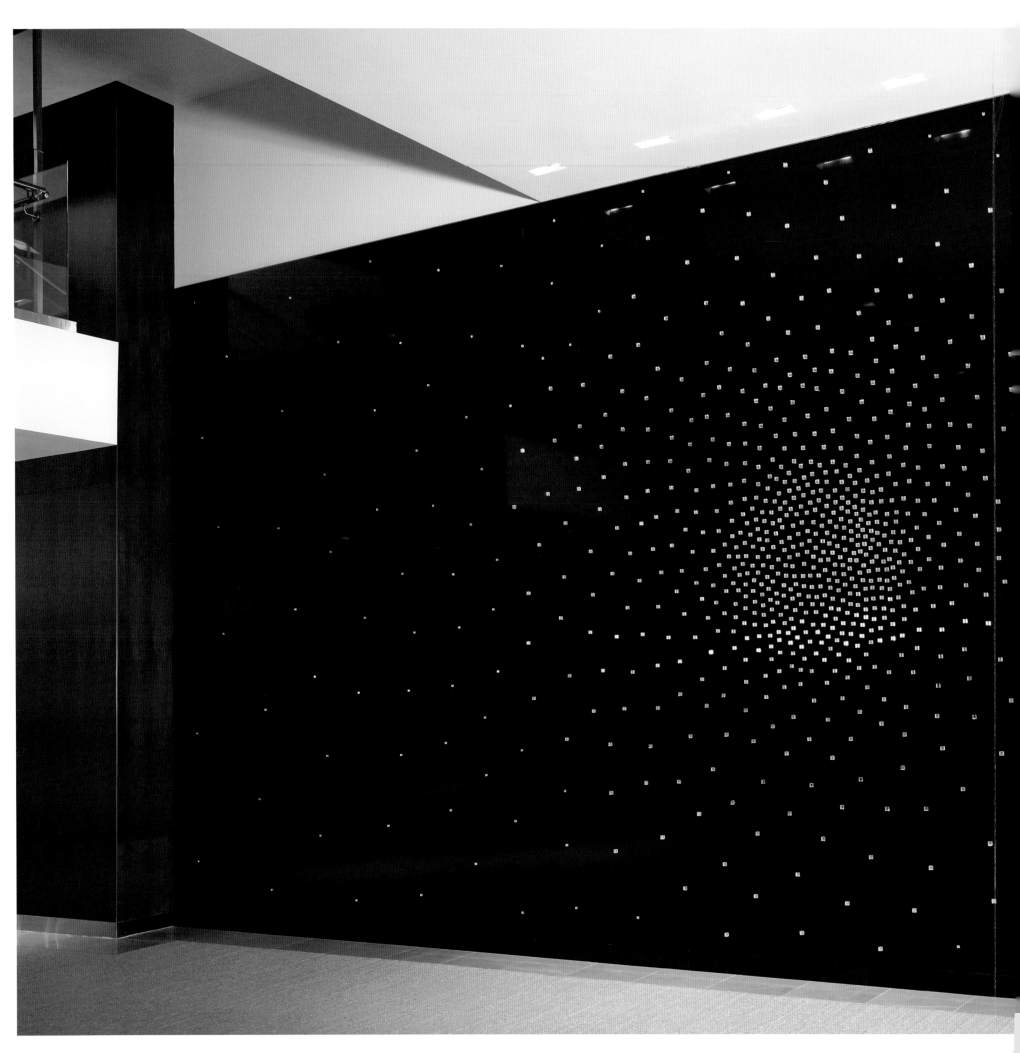

TERESITA FERNÁNDEZ
STARFIELD (2009)

Mirrored glass cubes on anodized aluminum
Approximately 14 feet by 31 feet
Site-specific commission
LOCATED ON HALL OF FAME LEVEL, SOUTHWEST ELEVATOR LOBBY

In the 1960s, Minimalism stripped art down to the basics: simple shapes, standard materials, and viewers, who were often puzzled by its stubborn silence. Since then, Minimalism has matured, becoming more refined, less abrasive, more gracious. Teresita Fernández, a New York artist of Cuban descent, takes Minimalism to elegant heights, creating accessible installations that fill the seemingly empty space between things with a sensual charge that transforms otherwise incidental details into evocations of infinity.

In terms of composition and materials, Fernández's *Starfield* (2009) could not be simpler: bright dots of light cluster in the center of a glossy black wall. Think disco ball flattened by a steamroller. Hold that image in mind while picturing the serene beauty of a crystal-clear night sky in the middle of nowhere, where so many stars twinkle that one cannot help but be awed by the vastness of the cosmos and our tiny place in it. Together, the two images suggest the magic Fernández works in her installation, which is made of nothing but hundreds of mirrored glass

cubes (about the size of ice cubes) and sheets of black laminate that cover the wall. The most important element, however, is the space between *Starfield* and the viewer—and what happens in it.

In every tiny mirror, one sees a miniature reflection. Stepping back, a ghostly silhouette appears on the dark surface. But the best things happen when one keeps moving like a star in the sky. That is when Fernández's art comes alive, twinkling, shimmering, and reflecting all the colors of the spectrum. Like a rainbow, you cannot touch it or keep it or forget seeing it.

MEL BOCHNER
WIN! (2009)

Acrylic on wall
Approximately 38 feet by 33 feet
Site-specific commission
LOCATED IN NORTHEAST MONUMENTAL STAIRCASE

Mel Bochner uses words in the same way that a painter uses colors—to get the viewer to see subtle differences between similar things.

Win! (2009) begins simply, with the word for what every fan wants his team to do, whether he's screaming it on Sunday or reading it in the headlines of Monday's paper. Simplicity disappears with the next word: "Vanquish" takes "win" to extremes, suggesting the overpowering of an utterly defeated foe. "Conquer" adds notions of control and possession to the rapidly growing mixture of meanings. Then "Clobber!" "Drub!" and "Rout!" evoke the exaggerated language of comic strips as they also recall the clichés often typed by sportswriters.

At this point, the viewer has only made it through one-quarter of Bochner's surprisingly dense work. To read the rest, which takes less than ten seconds, is to see the language get increasingly colorful—eventually taking on a life of its own.

Win! is the biggest work in Bochner's ongoing series of "Thesaurus Paintings." This body of work focuses on the ways language both conveys and derails meaning. Bochner has used words in his works since the late 1960s, when, as an original member of the Conceptual art movement, he became fascinated with their power and mystery.

Unlike sporting contests, which end with the black-and-white clarity of a win or a loss, Bochner's pedestrian poetry takes us into the gray areas, where shades of meaning are as important to the message as what it literally communicates.

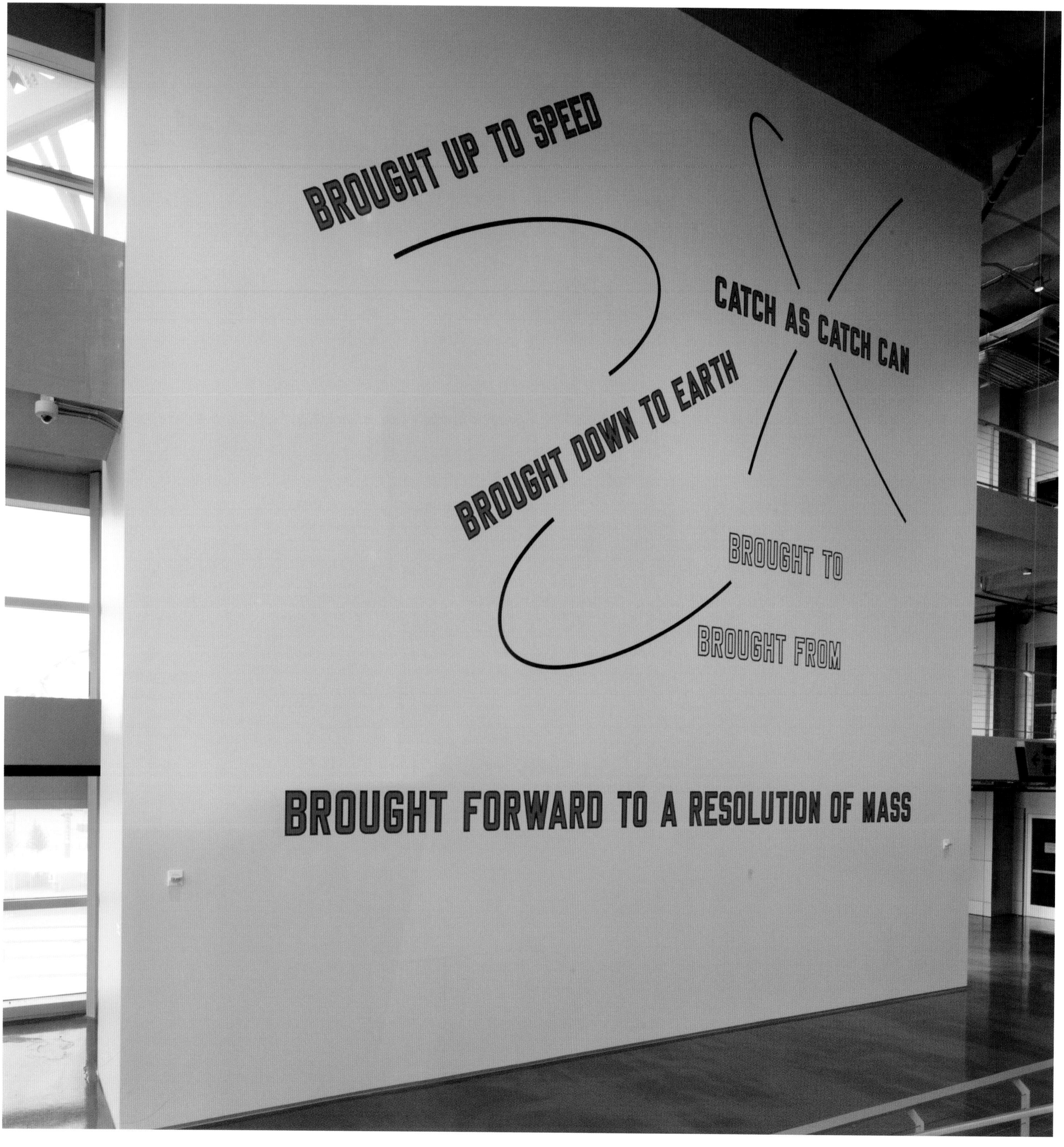

BROUGHT UP TO SPEED
CATCH AS CATCH CAN
BROUGHT DOWN TO EARTH
BROUGHT TO
BROUGHT FROM
BROUGHT FORWARD TO A RESOLUTION OF MASS

LAWRENCE WEINER
BROUGHT UP TO SPEED (2009)

LANGUAGE + MATERIALS REFERRED TO
Approximately 38 feet by 33 feet
Site-specific commission
LOCATED IN SOUTHWEST MONUMENTAL STAIRCASE

Anyone who knows how to read street signs will be able to understand Lawrence Weiner's *BROUGHT UP TO SPEED* (2009). No insider information is necessary to get what matters from this mural-sized wall-work: the ideas it generates, the feelings that accompany them, and the conversations that follow.

Weiner was one of the founding fathers of Conceptual art. This internationally renowned movement began with the belief that objects of art are less important than the impressions they make on viewers, who are free to take these impressions with them—and free to take them as far as they desire. Such populist commitments have been essential to Weiner's art since 1968, when he stopped making paintings and began using stencils to write brief statements directly on the wall.

Here, Weiner's piece features phrases people use every day: "brought up to speed," "brought down to earth," and "catch as catch can." They call to mind highlights of past games that are still vivid memories: say, a rookie learning on the job; the thump of a bone-crunching tackle; and a speedy receiver making an acrobatic catch.

Weiner's words also invite visitors to anticipate moments that have not yet happened on the field—to look forward to more excitement in the future. That is the beauty of language. If it captures your imagination, it can be used over and over again, by thousands and thousands of people, without wearing out or losing its punch.

GARY SIMMONS
BLUE FIELD EXPLOSIONS (2009)

Urethane, pigment, and oil stick on wall
Approximately 22 feet by 70 feet
Site-specific commission
LOCATED IN NORTHEAST MONUMENTAL STAIRCASE

On any given Sunday, everything can change in a split second. That is why big plays, explosive hits, even questionable calls are so important to sports: with them, momentum shifts, games turn, and winners rise above losers.

Gary Simmons's gigantic wall drawing captures the energy of these decisive moments. Rather than depicting a specific event and limiting his art to illustrating the past, Simmons brings the sudden, ear-splitting, earth-shattering, outcome-altering explosiveness of game highlights into the present, where viewers are called on to fill in the blanks by using their imaginations. Kids do it all the time. And part of the power of *Blue Field Explosions* (2009) is that it reawakens, in adults, the capacity to anticipate, to dream, and to hope.

Simmons emerged as an artist in the early 1990s with his "Erasure Drawings," a series of chalk drawings on blackboards. An African-American, he began many of these works by accurately outlining 1930s cartoon characters that often embodied racial stereotypes. Simmons then used his bare hands, arms, and shoulders to smudge, smear, and all but erase the white-on-black images. What resulted were ghostly, gray traces of the original characters and the artist's unsuccessful yet vigorous, even violent, attempts to obliterate them.

The double-edged thrust continues in the double-barreled format of *Blue Field Explosions*. This huge, handmade drawing builds on the comic strip–inspired Pop Art of Andy Warhol and Roy Lichtenstein by making a place for the artist's touch in a world of mass-produced imagery. For Simmons, that is both subtle and tough, elegant and explosive.

FRANZ ACKERMANN
COMING HOME (2009)
(MEET ME) AT THE WATERFALL (2009)

Acrylic on wall
Coming Home: 24 feet by 70 feet
(Meet me) At the Waterfall (work spans two levels): 62 feet by 40 feet, and 15 feet by 131 feet
Site-specific commission
LOCATED IN SOUTHWEST MONUMENTAL STAIRCASE

Franz Ackermann began his artistic career by making "Mental Maps." No bigger than postcards, these colored-pencil drawings captured his memories of walks around Hong Kong. The German artist had moved there when he finished graduate school because he wanted to get the feel for an unfamiliar city without the benefit of knowing its language. Ultimately, his goal was to convey the rhythm of his trips around town abstractly, by means of color, line, and shape.

Since then, Ackermann has picked up the pace of his travels and increased the size of his works. His two gigantic murals, *Coming Home* and *(Meet me) At the Waterfall* (both 2009) started off as recollections of his journey from his hometown, Berlin, to the North Texas area, where he did even more sightseeing. Ackermann then made many drawings, watercolors, and paintings, all based on what he had seen. To translate these studies to the walls of the stadium he used projectors and a crew of eight assistants, all artists in their own right.

His pair of wraparound landscapes lets viewers experience the excitement of travel through the past and the present. Texas Stadium appears in the distance, a fond memory amid pulsating shapes and jazzy color combinations. To take in the magnificent murals is to take a trip, in the imagination, to a place never before visited. That's what painters Vasily Kandinsky and Franz Marc did at the beginning of the twentieth century. Ackermann updates their Expressionist abstractions, turning art into an urban adventure.

TODD EBERLE
STADIUM PORTFOLIO

photographs © 2009, 2010 Todd Eberle

As a photographer whose work is realistic, Todd Eberle's job sounds fairly simple: point the camera at an interesting subject, click the shutter, and print. But such thinking does not get at the magic that happens when Eberle makes a photograph. His pictures of people, places, and things that are often familiar, if not well-known, make us see the world differently—more fully, richly, and sensitively than if left to our own devices, habits, and manners.

As an artist, Eberle's subject is not the buildings, events, and celebrities that appear in his works; it is our perception of the world around us and our understanding of our place in it. Changing the way people see things has been one of art's jobs since the beginning of time, and the New York-based Eberle uses a camera, as well as his keen eye for light and exacting sense of timing, to achieve altered perceptions. His stunning images are often published in magazines and books, where they sometimes appear as pairs.

Today, more people see more pictures than ever before, and the information overload can result in diminished attention spans. Eberle's sharply focused pairs of photographs stand up against this trend by slowing us down, by making us see similarities between different things and search for connections that are not obvious, simple, or immediately revealed. Eberle gets us to savor ordinarily overlooked details and wonder what we would be missing, if not for the eye-opening beauty of his works in which nothing is made up, yet everything is different and more gorgeous—even glorious—than usual.

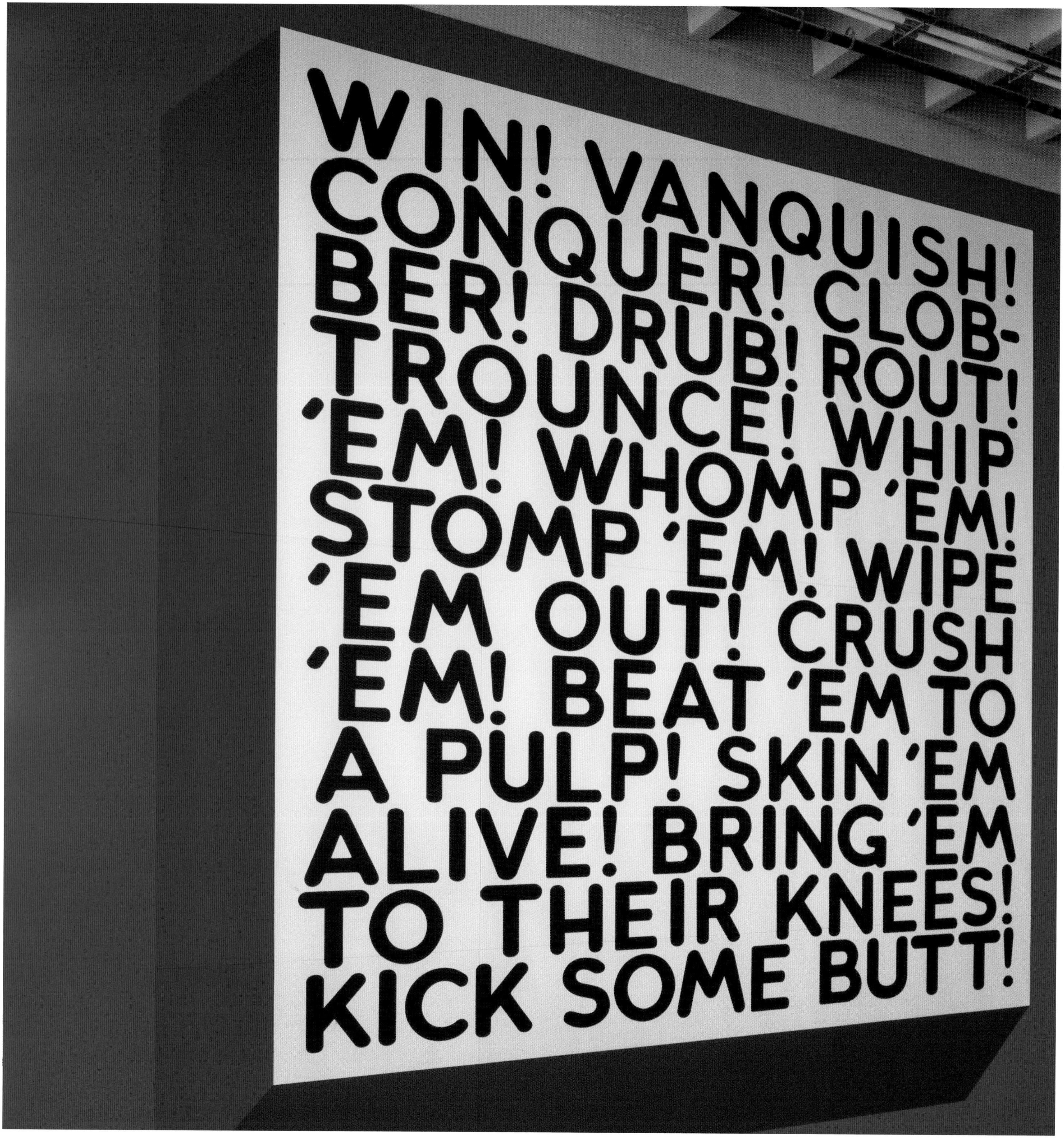
WIN! VANQUISH!
CONQUER! CLOB-
BER! DRUB! ROUT!
TROUNCE! WHIP
‘EM! WHOMP ‘EM!
STOMP ‘EM! WIPE
‘EM OUT! CRUSH
‘EM! BEAT ‘EM TO
A PULP! SKIN ‘EM
ALIVE! BRING ‘EM
TO THEIR KNEES!
KICK SOME BUTT!

28 FELIX JONES ★   ★ **9 TONY ROMO** ★   ★ **82 JASON WITTEN**

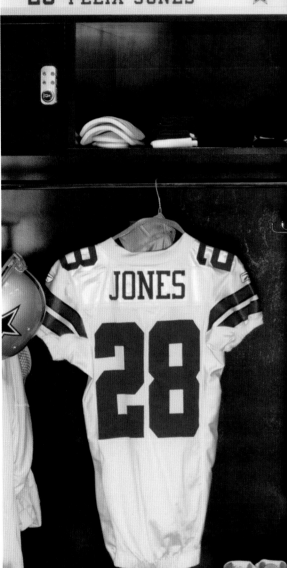

ENTERTAINMENT

THE EVENTS OF COWBOYS STADIUM

When designing Cowboys Stadium, the Jones family strived, from the beginning, to create more than a home for the Dallas Cowboys. Their dream was to build the next great architectural icon—a place that would appeal not only to fans of sports and entertainment but also to those of architecture, art, design, engineering, and technology. As a complete destination environment, Cowboys Stadium aspired to be much more than a boldly designed shell.

The result is a venue that has changed the way fans experience entertainment, by making every aspect of the event more thrilling, gracious, and awe-inspiring than ever before. This building, which scored international acclaim upon its opening, met those expectations and more, creating the grandest stage for athletes, musicians, and performers. NBC broadcaster Al Michaels proclaimed, "What the Roman Colosseum was to the first century, Cowboys Stadium is to the twenty-first century."

The stadium's cutting-edge technology and flexible interior spaces are easily adapted for diverse uses, and the digital media board suspended over the center of the field has revolutionized the way fans experience a live event. The building's sheer "wow" factor has already begun attracting a world of events and audiences. Even before the doors opened, Cowboys Stadium was slated to host some of the greatest sporting events: Super Bowl XLV, the 2010 NBA All-Star Game, and the 2014 NCAA Men's Final Four Basketball Championship. The stadium's versatility also has welcomed events that span the entertainment spectrum: soccer, concerts, high school and college football, professional bull riding, and boxing, to name just a few.

As a venue of this magnitude, one with the ability to shape itself to provide the ultimate in fan experience, Cowboys Stadium has welcomed audiences of all ages, demographics, and nationalities. Cowboys Stadium is the culmination of visionary leadership, historical precedent, and contemporary innovation that will change the way the world experiences sports and entertainment.

As a complete destination environment, Cowboys Stadium aspired to be much more than a boldly designed shell. The result is a venue that has changed the way fans experience entertainment, by making every aspect of the event more thrilling, gracious, and awe-inspiring than ever before.

DAVID DILLON

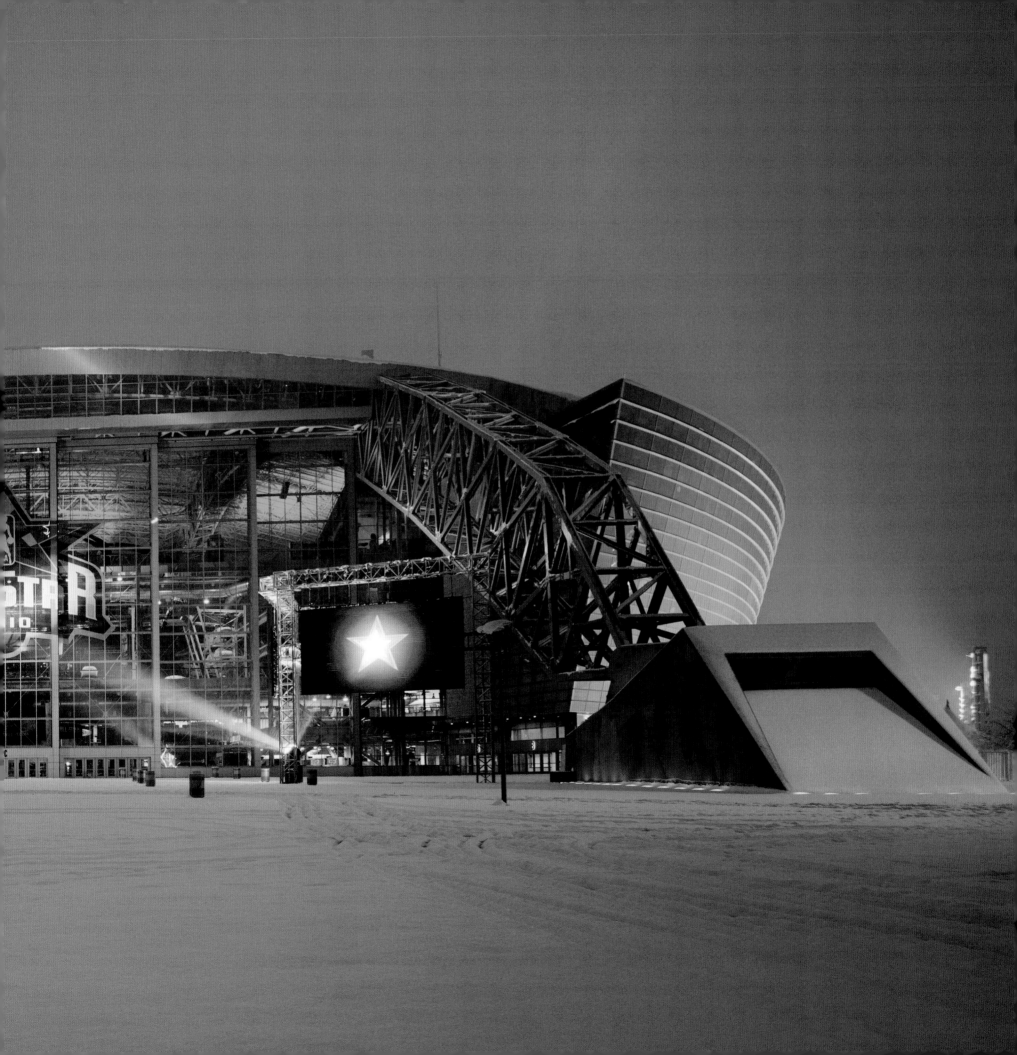

ARTISTS' BIOS

Franz Ackermann

Born 1964, Neumarkt St. Veit, Germany
Lives and works in Berlin and Karlsruhe, Germany

COMING HOME and (MEET ME) AT THE WATERFALL, 2009
Acrylic on wall
Coming Home: 24 feet by 70 feet
(Meet me) At the Waterfall (work spans two levels): 62 feet by
40 feet, and 15 feet by 131 feet
Site-specific commission
APPEARS ON PAGES 122–125

SELECTED EXHIBITIONS
2010 "Wait," White Cube, London **2009** "Altermodern: Tate
Triennial 2009," Tate Britain, London; "Franz Ackermann,"
Kunstmuseum Bonn, Germany; "Against the Grain,"
Kunstmuseum Wolfsburg, Germany; "Private Universes,"
Dallas Museum of Art, Dallas; "Desenhos: A a Z (Drawings A
to Z)," Museu da Cidade, Lisbon; "The Symbolic Efficiency of
the Frame," Tirana International Contemporary Art Biannual,
Albania **2008** "Franz Ackermann," Kunstmuseum St. Gallen,
Switzerland **2007** "Reality Bites—Making Avant-Garde Art
in Post-Wall Germany," Mildred Lane Kemper Art Museum,
St. Louis, Missouri **2006** "Berlin-Tokio / Tokio-Berlin," Neue
Nationalgalerie, Berlin and Mori Art Museum, Tokyo; "Satellite
of Love Witte de With," Rotterdam, The Netherlands; "The
Triumph of Painting," Saatchi Collection, London **2005** IMMA
Irish Museum of Modern Art, Dublin; "Ecstasy: In and About
Altered States," Museum of Contemporary Art, The Geffen
Contemporary, Los Angeles **2003** "Naherholungsgebiet,"
Kunstmuseum Wolfsburg, Germany **2002** "The Waterfall,"
Museum of Contemporary Art, Chicago; "Seasons in the Sun,"
Stedelijk Museum, Amsterdam **2000** "Franz Ackermann,"
Castello di Rivoli, Turin, Italy

Doug Aitken

Born 1968, Redondo Beach, California
Lives and works in Los Angeles, California

STAR, 2008
Neon-lit light box
45 inches by 119 inches by 10 inches
Edition 2 of 4
Acquisition
APPEARS ON PAGE 88

NEW HORIZON, 2009
LED-lit light box
66 inches by 70 inches by 8 1/4 inches
Edition 3 of 4
Acquisition
APPEARS ON PAGE 110

SELECTED EXHIBITIONS
2009 "Doug Aitken: No Sound," Aspen Art Museum, Aspen,
Colorado **2008** Carnegie International, Carnegie Museum of
Art, Pittsburgh, Pennsylvania **2007** "Doug Aitken: Sleepwalkers,"
Museum of Modern Art, New York **2006** "Doug Aitken," Aspen
Art Museum, Aspen, Colorado; "Doug Aitken," The Parrish
Art Museum, Southampton, New York; "Doug Aitken: Broken
Screen," Happenings, New York and Los Angeles **2005** "Doug
Aitken," Musée d'Art Moderne de la Ville de Paris **2004** "Doug
Aitken," Sammlung Goetz, Munich **2003** "Doug Aitken,"
Kunsthalle Zürich **2003** "Doug Aitken," Magasin—Centre
National d'Art Contemporain de Grenoble, France; "Doug
Aitken," Kunsthaus Bregenz, Louisiana Museum of Modern
Art, Humlebaek, Denmark **2001** "Doug Aitken," KW Institute
for Contemporary Art, Berlin; "Doug Aitken," Kunstmuseum
Wolfsburg, Germany **2000** "Doug Aitken: Glass Horizon,"

Secession, Vienna; "Doug Aitken: Matrix 185/Into the Sun," Berkeley Art Museum, Berkeley, California; "Concentrations 33: Doug Aitken, Diamond Sea," Dallas Museum of Art, Dallas

SELECTED AWARDS
2007 First Prize, German Film Critics' Award, KunstFilmBiennale, Cologne, Germany
2000 Aldrich Award, Aldrich Museum of Contemporary Art, Ridgefield, Connecticut
1999 Golden Lion, Venice Biennale, Venice, Italy

Ricci Albenda
Born 1966, New York, New York
Lives and works in New York, New York

INTERIOR LANDSCAPE, FULL SPECTRUM, 2009
Acrylic on aluminum panels
Approximately 21 feet by 131 feet
Site-specific commission
APPEARS ON PAGE 96

SELECTED EXHIBITIONS
2010 "Contemplating the Void: Interventions in the Guggenheim Museum," Guggenheim Museum, New York **2009** "The Quick Brown Fox Jumps over the Lazy Dog," Rachofsky House, Dallas **2008** "26 Devoe," The Horticultural Society of New York, New York; "Fighting Words," Fisher Landau Center for Art, Long Island City, New York **2007** "The Shapes of Space," Guggenheim Museum, New York **2006** "Supervision," Institute of Contemporary Art, Boston **2004** "Disparities and Deformations: Our Grotesque." SITE Santa Fe 5th International Biennial, Sante Fe, New Mexico; "Open House: Working in Brooklyn," Brooklyn Museum of Art **2003** "Warped Space," CCA Wattis Institute for Contemporary Arts, San Francisco; "The Moderns," curated by Carolyn Christov-Bakargiev, Castello Di Rivoli, Museo dí Arte Contemporanea, Torino, Italy **2002** "Out of Site," New Museum of Contemporary Art, New York **2001** "Projects 74: Ricci Albenda," Museum of Modern Art, New York **2000** "Ricci Albenda," Van Laere Contemporary Art, Antwerp, Belgium; "Greater New York," P.S.1 Contemporary Art Center, Museum of Modern Art, Long Island City, New York

SELECTED AWARDS
1999 The Louis Comfort Tiffany Biennial Award

Mel Bochner
Born 1940, Pittsburgh, Pennsylvania
Lives and works in New York, New York

WIN!, 2009
Acrylic on wall
Approximately 38 feet by 33 feet
Site-specific commission
APPEARS ON PAGE 116

SELECTED EXHIBITIONS
2008 "Genau und Anders," Museum Ludwig, Vienna **2007** "Lines, Grids, Stains, and Words," The Museum of Modern Art, New York; "Magritte and Contemporary Art: The Treachery of Images," Los Angeles County Museum of Art; "Live/Work: Performance into Drawing," The Museum of Modern Art, New York **2006** "The Joys of Yiddish," Spertus Museum, Chicago; "Focus: Mel Bochner—Language 1966–2006," The Art Institute of Chicago **2005** "Open Systems: Rethinking Art c. 1970," Tate Modern, London; "Building and Breaking the Grid," Whitney Museum of American Art, New York **2004** "A Minimal Future?" Los Angeles Museum of

Contemporary Art; Whitney Biennial, Whitney Museum of American Art, New York **2003** "Mel Bochner: Measurement Paintings," Musee d'Art Moderne et Contemporain, Geneva; "The Last Picture Show: Artists Using Photography 1960–1982," Walker Art Center, Minneapolis, Minnesota **2002** "Forum: Mel Bochner Photographs," Carnegie Museum of Art, Pittsburgh, Pennsylvania **2001** "As Painting, Division and Displacement," Wexner Center for the Arts, Columbus, Ohio **1999** "The American Century: Art and Culture 1900–2000 (Part II, 1950–2000)," Whitney Museum of American Art, New York **1997** "Mel Bochner," Musee d'art modern et contemporain, Geneva 1995 "1965–1995: Reconsidering the Object of Art," The Museum of Contemporary Art, Los Angeles **1987** "1967: At the Crossroads," Institute of Contemporary Art, University of Pennsylvania, Philadelphia **1986** "Mel Bochner, 1973–1985," Kunstmuseum, Lucerne, Switzerland **1983** "Minimalism to Expressionism," Whitney Museum of American Art, New York **1982** "74th American Exhibition," Chicago Art Institute, Chicago **1979** Whitney Biennial, Whitney Museum of American Art, New York; "The Decade in Review," Whitney Museum of American Art, New York **1977** Whitney Biennial, Whitney Museum of American Art, New York; "Ten Years," Museum of Contemporary Art, Chicago **1976** "Drawing Now," The Museum of Modern Art, New York **1972** Documenta 5, Kassel, Germany **1971** "Mel Bochner," The Museum of Modern Art, New York **1966** "Working drawings and other visible things on paper not necessarily meant to be viewed as art," School of Visual Arts Gallery, New York

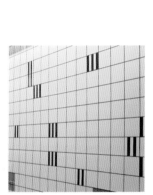

Daniel Buren
Born 1938, Boulogne-Billancourt, France
Lives and works *in situ*

UNEXPECTED VARIABLE CONFIGURATIONS: A WORK IN SITU, 1998
Wall painted yellow with hand-drawn grid and 50 screen-printed aluminum plates
Approximately 21 feet by 118 feet
Editions 10 of 15 and 11 of 15
Acquisition
APPEARS ON PAGE 98

SELECTED EXHIBITIONS
2009 "A Mancha Humana / The Human Stain" Centro Galego de Arte Contemporánea (CGAC), Santiago de Compostela, Spain **2007** "New Situated Works," Lisson Gallery, London **2006** "Daniel Buren: Intervention II, Works in Situ," Modern Art Oxford **2005** "The Eye of the Storm: Works in Situ by Daniel Buren," Guggenheim Museum, New York; International Triennial of Contemporary Art, Yokohama, Japan **2003** "Transitions: Works in Situ," Municipal Museum of Art, Toyota, Japan **2002** "Le Musée qui n'exista it pas, works in situ," Centre Pompidou, Paris **1996** "Transparency of the Light," Art Tower Mito, Mito, Japan **1999** "Modulation Works in situ," Neues Museum Weserburg, Bremen, Germany **1991** "Daniel Buren, Arguments topiques," CAPC Musée d'Art Contemporain, Bordeaux, France **1989** Tokyo Museum of Contemporary Art, Tokyo; ICA, Nagoya, Japan **1988** "Daniel Buren: The Reverberation," The Brooklyn Museum, New York **1975/1979/1980/1983/1998/1999/2004/2005** "Toile/Voile–Voile/Toile," regattas followed by a museum presentation of Voiles-Toiles in Berlin, Geneva, Lucerne, Thun, Velleneuve d'Ascq, Lyon-Villeurbanne, Tel-Aviv, Seville, Grasmere **1973** Museum of Modern Art, Oxford **1972/1974/1976/1978/1980/1984/1986/1993/1997/2003/2007** Venice Biennale, Venice, Italy **1972/1977/1982** Documenta, Kassel **1971** Painting-Sculpture, censored work at the 6th Guggenheim International, Guggenheim Museum, New York

SELECTED AWARDS
1992 Grand Prix National de Peinture, Paris
1991 International Award for Best Artist, The Bad Wurtemberg Land, Stuttgart, Germany
1990 "Living Treasure" prize awarded by New Zealand
1986 Golden Lion, Best Pavilion, Venice Biennale
1965 Grand Prix of the Paris Biennial; Prix Lefranc of Young Painting

Bonn, Germany 2005 "Notion Motion," Museum Boijmans van Beuningen, Rotterdam, The Netherlands 2004 "Olafur Eliasson: Your Lighthouse," Kunstmuseum Wolfsburg, Germany 2003 50th Venice Biennale, Venice; "Olafur Eliasson: The Weather Project," Tate Modern, London 2002 "Chaque matin je me sens different…," Musée d'Art Moderne de la Ville de Paris 2001 "Olafur Eliasson: Seeing Yourself Sensing," Museum of Modern Art, New York 2000 "Olafur Eliasson: The Curious Garden," Irish Museum of Modern Art, Dublin

Todd Eberle
Born 1963, Cleveland, Ohio
Lives and works in New York, New York, and Connecticut

PHOTOGRAPHY APPEARS ON PAGES 126–135

SELECTED EXHIBITIONS
2009 "America," Light & Sie Gallery, Dallas, Texas; "Vortexhibition Polyphonica," Henry Art Gallery, Seattle, Washington; "Vanity Fair: The Portraits," National Portrait Gallery, Canberra, Australia 2008 "Hi-Fi + wired," Gallery White Room, Tokyo; "That Was Then … This Is Now," P.S.1 Contemporary Art Center, Museum of Modern Art, Long Island City, New York; "Other People: Portraits from Grunewald and Hammer Collections," UCLA Hammer Museum, Los Angeles; "Vanity Fair: The Portraits," Los Angeles County Museum of Art and the National Portrait Gallery, London 2007 "Todd Eberle," Gagosian Gallery, Beverly Hills, California 2006 "Architectural Abstractions," The Art Institute of Chicago; "Skin + Bones: Parallel Practices in Fashion and Architecture," The Los Angeles Museum of Contemporary Art 2005 "Robert Smithson Retrospective," Whitney Museum of American Art, New York; "Landscape/Cityscape," Marlborough Gallery, New York 2004 "Hi-Fi," P.S.1 Contemporary Art Center, Museum of Modern Art, Long Island City, New York; "Donald Judd," Tate Modern, London; "Glamour," San Francisco Museum of Modern Art 2001 "wired + Dan Flavin untitled (Marfa Project)," Galerie Thaddeus Ropac, Paris

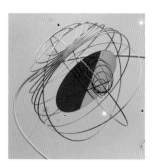

Olafur Eliasson
Born 1967, Copenhagen, Denmark
Lives and works in Berlin, Germany

MOVING STARS TAKES TIME, 2008
Stainless steel, polished stainless steel, glass mirror, color-effect filter glass, color foil, powder-coated steel, steel cable
Approximate dimensions spanning: 25 feet by 45 feet by 20 feet
Site-specific commission
APPEARS ON PAGE 82

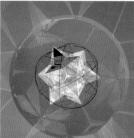

FAT SUPER STAR, 2008–09
Brass, color-effect filter glass, mirror, halogen light fixture
39 3/8 inches by 39 3/8 inches by 39 3/8 inches
Edition 2 of 10
Acquisition
APPEARS ON PAGE 104

SELECTED EXHIBITIONS
2009–07 "Olafur Eliasson: Take Your Time," San Francisco Museum of Modern Art, San Francisco, P.S.1 Contemporary Art Center, Museum of Modern Art, Long Island City, New York, Dallas Museum of Art, Dallas, Museum of Contemporary Art, Chicago, Museum of Contemporary Art, Sydney 2008 "Olafur Eliasson: The Nature of Things," Fundació Joan Miró, Barcelona 2006 "Olafur Eliasson: Remagine," Kunstmuseum

Teresita Fernández
Born 1968, Miami, Florida
Lives and works in New York, New York

STARFIELD, 2009
Mirrored glass cubes on anodized aluminum
Approximately 14 feet by 31 feet
Site-specific commission
APPEARS ON PAGE 114

SELECTED EXHIBITIONS
2009 "Blind Landscape," Contemporary Art Museum, University of South Florida, Tampa, and Blanton Museum of Art, Austin, Texas 2007 "Sculptors Drawing," Aspen Art Museum, Aspen, Colorado 2006 "Big Juicy Paintings (and More): Selections from the Permanent Collection," Miami Art Museum, Miami, Florida 2005 "MoCA & Miami," Museum of Contemporary Art, Miami, Florida; "Extreme Abstraction," Albright-Knox Gallery, Buffalo, New York; Centro de Arte Contemporáneo de Málaga, Spain 2004 "In Situ: Installations and Large-Scale Works in the Permanent Collection," Museum of Contemporary Art, Miami 2002 "Outer City, Inner Space: Teresita Fernández, Stephen Hendee, and Ester Partegas," Whitney Philip Morris, New York; "The Young Latins," Nassau County Museum of Art, Long Island, New York 2001 "Globe<Miami>Island," Bass Museum of Art, Miami, Florida; "Hortus Conclusus," Witte de With, Rotterdam, The Netherlands; "Inside Space," MIT List Visual Arts Center, Cambridge, Massachusetts; "Reading the Museum," The National Museum of Modern Art, Tokyo, Japan 2000 "Wonderland," St. Louis Art Museum, St. Louis, Missouri; "Greater New York," P.S.1 Contemporary Art Center, Museum of Modern Art, Long Island City, New York; "Hothouse," Museum of Modern Art, New York; "Teresita Fernández, Roni Horn, Mona Hatoum," SITE Santa Fe, Santa Fe, New Mexico; "Supernova," Berkeley Art Museum/Matrix, Berkeley, California

SELECTED AWARDS
2005 MacArthur Foundation Fellowship
2003 Guggenheim Fellowship
1999 Louis Comfort Tiffany Biennial Award

Wayne Gonzales
Born 1957, New Orleans, Louisiana
Lives and works in New York, New York

CHEERING CROWD, 2007
Acrylic on canvas, triptych
7 feet by 21 feet
Acquisition
APPEARS ON PAGE 112

SELECTED EXHIBITIONS
2009 "Every Revolution is a Roll of the Dice," Paula Cooper Gallery, New York 2008 "Ithaca Collects," Herbert F. Johnson

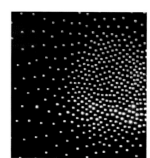

Museum of Art, Ithaca, New York **2007** "Judge: Vincent Katz and Wayne Gonzales," Paula Cooper Gallery, New York; "Currents: Recent Acquisitions," Hirshhorn Museum and Sculpture Garden, Washington, D.C.; "A Roll of the Dice Will Never Abolish Chance," Marfa Ballroom, Marfa, Texas; "Remix the Collection," Albright-Knox Art Gallery, Buffalo, New York; "Resistance Is," Whitney Museum of American Art, New York **2006** "Project.3—Wayne Gonzales," Mason Gross Galleries, Rutgers University, New Brunswick, New Jersey **2005** "The Painted World," P.S.1 Center for Contemporary Art, Museum of Modern Art, Long Island City, New York

Arts Museum, Houston, The Modern Art Museum of Fort Worth, Texas, and Texas Fine Arts Association at the Jones Center for Contemporary Art, Austin, Texas

SELECTED AWARDS

2007 Joyce Alexander Wein Award, The Studio Museum in Harlem, New York
2004 Penny McCall Foundation Award
2003 Artadia Foundation Award
1999 Joan Mitchell Foundation, Grant Recipient

Terry Haggerty
Born 1970, London, UK
Lives and works in New York and Berlin, Germany

TWO MINDS, 2009
Acrylic on wall
Approximately 21 feet by 126 feet
Site-specific commission
APPEARS ON PAGE 94

SELECTED EXHIBITIONS
2010 Andreas Grimm, München, Germany **2009** Center for Contemporary Non-Objective Art, Brussels, Belgium; "Connected Things Collected," Sammlung Haubrok, Berlin **2008** "Lose Track," PS Project Space, Amsterdam; "International and National Projects Fall 2008," P.S.1 Contemporary Art Center, Museum of Modern Art, Long Island City, New York; "Something and Something Else," Museum van Bommel van Dam, Venlo, The Netherlands **2007** "Hammer Projects," UCLA Hammer Museum, Los Angeles; "Machine Learning," Painting Center, New York **2004** "Incognito," Santa Monica Museum of Art, Santa Monica **2003** "The Peripheries Become the Center: Prague Biennale 1," Czechoslovakia **2001** "Best of Season," The Aldrich Contemporary Art Museum, Ridgefield, Connecticut

SELECTED AWARDS

1999 Natwest Art Prize, London

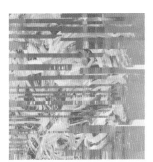

Jacqueline Humphries
Born 1960, New Orleans, Louisiana
Lives and works in New York, New York

BLONDNOIR, 2008
Oil and enamel on linen
90 inches by 96 inches
Acquisition
APPEARS ON PAGE 100

SELECTED EXHIBITIONS
2009 "Jacqueline Humphries," Greene Naftali Gallery, New York **2008** Prospect.1 New Orleans, curated by Dan Cameron **2007** "Jacqueline Humphries," Stuart Shave/Modern Art, London; "Affinities: Painting in Abstraction," CCS Bard Hessel Museum, Annadale-on-Hudson, New York **2006** "Jacqueline Humphries: New Work," Williams College Museum of Art, Williamstown, Massachusetts **2004** "Selections from the Collection of the Museum of Fine Arts, Boston," Nagoya Museum, Japan **2001** "Against the Wall: Painting Against the Grid, Surface and Frame," Institute of Contemporary Art, Philadelphia

SELECTED AWARDS

1999 Pollock Krasner Foundation Grant
1995 Joan Mitchell Foundation Grant
1992 Louis Comfort Tiffany Award

Trenton Doyle Hancock
Born 1974, Oklahoma City, Oklahoma
Lives and works in Houston, Texas

FROM A LEGEND TO A CHOIR, 2009
Vinyl print
Approximately 40 feet by 98 feet
Site-specific commission
APPEARS ON PAGE 108

SELECTED EXHIBITIONS
2008 "Trenton Doyle Hancock," Institute of Contemporary Art, Philadelphia, Pennsylvania **2007** "The Wayward Thinker," The Fruitmarket Gallery, Edinburgh, Scotland; Museum Boijmans Van Beuningen, Rotterdam, The Netherlands **2006** "The Compulsive Line: Etching 1900 to Now," Museum of Modern Art, New York; "Black Alphabet," Zacheta National Gallery of Art, Warsaw, Poland **2004** "Perspectives@25: A Quarter-Century of New Art in Houston," Contemporary Arts Museum, Houston; "Political Nature," Whitney Museum of American Art, New York **2003** "Poetic Justice," 8th International Istanbul Biennial, Istanbul, Turkey; "It Happened Tomorrow," 7th Lyon Biennale of Contemporary Art, Lyon, France; "Moments in Mound History," The Cleveland Museum of Art, Cleveland, Ohio **2002** Whitney Biennial, Whitney Museum of American Art, New York **2001** "The Life and Death of #1," Contemporary

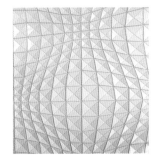

Jim Isermann
Born 1955, Kenosha, Wisconsin
Lives and works in Palm Springs, California

UNTITLED, 2009-10
Vacuum-formed styrene wall
40 feet by 96 feet
Site-specific commission
APPEARS ON PAGE 106

SELECTED EXHIBITIONS
2006 "Jim Isermann," Museum of Contemporary Art, Chicago; "Unit Structures," organized by Pablo Lafuente for Lisboa 20, Lisbon, Portugal **2005** "Extreme Abstraction," Albright Knox Art Gallery, Buffalo; "Faces in the Crowd: Picturing Modern Life from Manet to Today," Castello di Rivoli, Turin, Italy; "Icestorm," Kunstverein, Munich **2002** "Hammer Projects," UCLA Hammer Museum, Los Angeles; "The Gallery Show," Royal Academy of Fine Art, London; "Trespassing: Houses by Artists," The Bellevue Art Museum, Bellevue, Washington and MAK Center for Art and Architecture, Los Angeles **2001** "Beau Monde: Toward a Redeemed Cosmopolitanism," SITE Santa Fe 4th International Biennial, Santa Fe, New Mexico; "The Magic Hour," Neue Galerie, Graz, Austria; "Tele(visions)," Kunsthalle Wien, Vienna **2000** "Made in California: Now,"

Los Angeles County Museum of Art; "What If?" Modern Museum, Stockholm, Sweden.

SELECTED AWARDS
2001 Guggenheim Fellowship
1987 National Endowment for the Arts, Visual Artist's Fellowship, Painting
1984 National Endowment for the Arts, Visual Artist's Fellowship, Sculpture

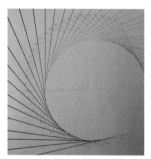

Annette Lawrence
Born 1965, Rockville Centre, New York
Lives and works in Denton, Texas

COIN TOSS, 2009
Stranded cable
14 feet diameter by approximately 45 feet (span)
Site-specific commission
APPEARS ON PAGE 84

SELECTED EXHIBITIONS
2009 "On the Body: Selected Work from the Rachofsky Collection," The University of North Texas Art Gallery, Denton, Texas **2008** "Learning by Doing: 25 Years of the Core Program at the Museum of Fine Arts, Houston (Part II)," The Museum of Fine Arts, Houston; "Houston Collects," The Museum of Fine Arts, Houston; "Lone Star Legacy II: The Barrett Collection of Contemporary Texas Art," Dallas Museum of Art, Dallas **2006** "The Collection in Context: Gesture," The Studio Museum in Harlem, New York **2005** "Double Consciousness: Black Conceptual Art Since 1970," Contemporary Arts Museum, Houston; "Pairings," Dallas Center for Contemporary Art, Dallas **2004** "Perspectives@25: A Quarter-Century of New Art in Houston," Contemporary Arts Museum, Houston; "African-American Art from the MFAH Collection," Museum of Fine Arts, Houston **2000** "Next Text," Arlington Museum of Art, Arlington, Texas

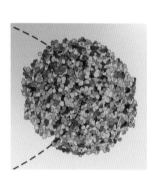

Dave Muller
Born 1964, San Francisco, California
Lives and works in Los Angeles, California

SOLAR ARRANGEMENT, 2009
Acrylic on wall
Approximately 21 feet by 131 feet
Site-specific commission
APPEARS ON PAGE 92

SELECTED EXHIBITIONS
2009 "Rock – Paper – Scissors: Pop Music as Subject of Visual Art," Kunsthaus Graz, Austria **2008** "Sandra and Gerald Fineberg Art Wall," The Institute of Contemporary Art, Boston; "Jeremy Deller: Marlon Brando, Pocahontas and Me," Aspen Art Museum, Aspen, Colorado **2007** "Sympathy for the Devil: Art and Rock and Roll Since 1967," Museum of Contemporary Art, Chicago **2005** 8th Biennale d'Art Contemporain de Lyon 2005, Lyon, France **2004** "New Work: Evan Holloway and Dave Muller," San Francisco Museum of Modern Art; "A Molecular History of Everything," Australian Center for Contemporary Art, Victoria; Whitney Biennial, Whitney Museum of American Art, New York **2003** "It Happened Tomorrow," 7th

Lyon Biennale of Contemporary Art, Lyon, France; "Comic Release: Negotiating Identity for a New Generation," Carnegie Mellon University, Pittsburgh, Pennsylvania **2002** "Dave Muller: Connections," Center for Curatorial Studies Museum, Bard College, Annandale-on-Hudson, New York **2001** "Current 85, Dave Muller: Spatial," St. Louis Art Museum, Missouri

Matthew Ritchie
Born 1964, London, UK
Lives and works in New York

LINE OF PLAY, 2009
Powder-coated aluminum, vinyl, acrylic
East Wall, West Wall: 30 feet by 20 feet
Ceiling: 34 feet by 10 feet
Site-specific commission
APPEARS ON PAGE 86

SELECTED EXHIBTIONS
2008 "Biennale Architecture: 11th International Architecture Exhibition," Venice, Italy; "Out There: Architecture Beyond Building"; "Experiment Marathon Reykjavík," Reykjavík Art Museum; "The Guggenheim Collection," Guggenheim Bilbao, Spain **2007** "The Shapes of Space," Guggenheim Museum, New York; "Not For Sale," P.S.1 Contemporary Art Center, Museum of Modern Art, Long Island City, New York; "New Media Series: Matthew Ritchie, The Iron City," St. Louis Art Museum, Missouri **2006** "The Guggenheim Collection," Kunstmuseum Bonn, Germany **2005** "Remote Viewing: Invented Worlds in Recent Painting and Drawing," Whitney Museum of American Art, New York **2004** "Matthew Ritchie: Proposition Player," Massachusetts Museum of Contemporary Art, North Adams, Massachusetts; "São Paolo Biennial XXVI," São Paolo, Brazil 2003 "Matthew Ritchie: Proposition Player," Contemporary Arts Museum, Houston **2002** "(The World May Be) Fantastic: Biennale of Sydney 2002," Sydney, Australia **2001** "All Systems Go," Contemporary Arts Museum, Houston; "010101: Art in Technological Times," San Francisco Museum of Modern Art, San Francisco **2000** "Concentrations 38: Matthew Ritchie," The Dallas Museum of Art, Dallas

Eva Rothschild
Born 1971, Dublin, Ireland
Lives and works in London, UK

DIAMONOID, 2009
Powder-coated aluminum, Plexiglas
70 inches by 110 inches by 7 1/2 inches
Edition 1 of 3
Acquisition
APPEARS ON PAGE 90

SELECTED EXHIBITIONS
2009 "Eva Rothschild," Duveen Galleries, Tate Britain, London; "Eva Rothschild," Stuart Shave/Modern Art, London; "La Conservera," Centro de Arte Contemporaneo, Murcia, Spain; "The Dark Monarch," Tate St. Ives, Cornwall, UK **2008** Tate Britain, Millbank, London; The Modern Institute, Glasgow **2007** "Un-monumental: Falling to Pieces in the 21st Century," The New Museum of Contemporary Art, New York **2006** "All Hawaii Entrées / Lunar Reggae," Irish Museum of Modern

Art, Dublin; "How to Improve the World: 60 Years of British Art," Arts Council Collection, Hayward Gallery, London; The 3rd Tate Triennial, Tate Britain, London **2005** "Extreme Abstraction," Albright Knox Museum, Buffalo, New York **2004** "Eva Rothschild," Kunsthalle, Zurich; "Eva Rothschild," Artspace, Sydney, Australia **2003** "Heavy Cloud," The Modern Institute, Glasgow; The Carnegie International, The Carnegie Museum of Art, Pittsburgh, Pennsylvania

Gary Simmons

Born 1964, New York, New York
Lives and works in New York, New York

BLUE FIELD EXPLOSIONS, 2009
Urethane, pigment, and oil stick on wall
Approximately 22 feet by 70 feet
Site-specific commission
APPEARS ON PAGE 120

SELECTED EXHIBITIONS
2009 "NeoHooDoo: Art of a Forgotten Faith," Miami Art Museum, Miami, Florida; "30 Seconds Off an Inch," The Studio Museum in Harlem, New York; "Collecting History: Highlighting Recent Acquisitions," The Museum of Contemporary Art, Los Angeles; "Sites," Whitney Museum of American Art, New York **2008** "30 Americans," The Rubell Family Collection, Miami, Florida; Gwangju Biennale, Korea; "NeoHooDoo: Art for a Forgotten Faith," The Menil Collection, Houston **2007** "For the Love of the Game: Race and Sport in America," Wadsworth Atheneum Museum of Art, Hartford, Connecticut; "Comic Abstraction: Image-Breaking, Image-Making," The Museum of Modern Art, New York; **2005** "Double Consciousness: Black Conceptual Art Since 1970," Contemporary Arts Museum, Houston; "Past, Presence, Childhood and Memory," Whitney Museum of American Art at Altria, New York **2003** "Supernova: Art of the 1990s from the Logan Collection," San Francisco Museum of Modern Art, San Francisco **2001** "I'm Thinking of a Place," UCLA Hammer Museum, Los Angeles; "One Planet Under a Groove: Hip Hop and Contemporary Art," Bronx Museum, New York and Walker Art Center, Minneapolis, Minnesota

SELECTED AWARDS
2007 USA Gund Fellowship
1991 Penny McCall Foundation Grant
1990 National Endowment for the Arts Interarts Grant

Lawrence Weiner

Born 1942, New York, New York
Lives and works in New York, New York
and Amsterdam, The Netherlands

BROUGHT UP TO SPEED, 2009
LANGUAGE + MATERIALS REFERRED TO
Approximately 38 feet by 33 feet
Site-specific commission
APPEARS ON PAGE 118

SELECTED EXHIBITIONS
2009 "The Other Side of a Cul-de-Sac," The Power Plant, Toronto, Ontario; "Text/Messages: Books by Artists," Walker Art Center, Minneapolis, Minnesota; "REGIFT," Swiss

Institute, New York **2008** "As Far as the Eye Can See," Museum of Contemporary Art, Los Angeles, and K21 Kunstsammlung Nordhein-Westfalen, Dusseldorf, Germany; "The Crest of a Wave," Fundació Suñol, Barcelona, Spain; "Order. Desire. Light: An Exhibition of Contemporary Drawings," Irish Museum of Modern Art (IMMA), Dublin **2007** "As Far as the Eye Can See," The Whitney Museum of American Art, New York; 52nd International Art Exhibition of La Biennale di Venezia, Venice, Italy **2006** "Lawrence Weiner," Tate Modern, London **2004** "Covered by Clouds/Cubierto por Nubes," Tamayo Museum, Mexico City **2002** "Until It Is," Wexner Center for the Arts, Columbus, Ohio **2001** "Bent and Broken Shafts of Light," Kunstmuseum Wolfsburg, Germany **1999** "The American Century: Art and Culture (1950–2000)," Whitney Museum of American Art, New York **1995** Philadelphia Museum of Art, Philadelphia, Pennsylvania; Biennial 4, Istanbul Foundation for Culture and Arts, Istanbul, Turkey; Whitney Biennial, Whitney Museum of American Art, New York **1994** "Posters," Walker Art Center, Minneapolis, Minnesota **1992** San Francisco Museum of Modern Art, San Francisco **1991** "Displacement," CAPC Musée d'Art Contemporain de Bourdeaux, France; "Displacement," Dia Center for the Arts, New York **1990** "With the Passage of Time," Hirshhorn Museum and Sculpture Garden, Washington, D.C. **1985** Musé de Art Contemporain, Lyon, France **1984** Venice Biennale, Venice **1982** Documenta 7, Kassel, Germany **1980** Museum of Contemporary Art, Chicago **1978** Renaissance Society, University of Chicago, Chicago; "Special One-Day Exhibition of Four Art Language Video Tapes," Gallery Theatrette, Art Gallery of New South Wales, Sydney, Australia **1977** Salle Simon L. Patiño, Centre d'Art Contemporain, Geneva, Switzerland **1976** Institute for Contemporary Art, London **1972** Venice Biennale, Venice, Italy; Dokumenta 5, Kassel, Germany

SELECTED AWARDS
1994 John Simon Guggenheim Fellowship, New York
1988 Singer Prize, Singer Museum, Laren, The Netherlands
1983/1976 National Endowment for the Arts Fellowship, Washington, D.C.
1976 72nd American Exhibition, Art Institute of Chicago, prize, Chicago, Illinois

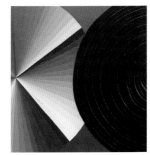

Garth Weiser

Born 1979, Helena, Montana
Lives and works in New York, New York

TV KEITH, 2008
Acrylic and gouache on canvas
93 inches by 83 inches
Acquisition
APPEARS ON PAGE 102

SELECTED EXHIBITIONS
2010 "Garth Weiser," Altman Siegel Gallery, San Francisco **2009** "Garth Weiser," Casey Kaplan, New York; "Changing Light Bulbs in Thin Air," Hessel Museum of Art & CCS Galleries, Annandale-on-Hudson, New York **2008** "Recent Acquisitions," Museum of Contemporary Art, Chicago; "The Triumph of Painting: Abstract America," Saatchi Gallery, London **2007** "First Hand Steroids," Andreas Melas Presents, Athens, Greece **2006** "Garth Weiser," Guild & Greyshkul, New York **2005** "Greater New York," P.S.1 Center for Contemporary Art, Museum of Modern Art, Long Island City, New York

THE AUTHORS

DAVID DILLON (1941-2010)

David Dillon was the architecture critic for the *Dallas Morning News* from 1983 to 2006, and taught in the Architecture School at the University of Massachusetts in Amherst. He was contributing editor to *Architectural Record* and wrote regularly for numerous national design and planning magazines. He authored ten books, including *Dallas Architecture 1936-1986*, *The Architecture of O'Neil Ford*, *The Miller Garden: Icon of Modernism*, and *Kallmann, McKinnell & Wood*. He was also the author of the new plan for Washington, D.C., *Extending the Legacy*, as well as the plan for the White House and President's Park.

David Dillon passed away before he was able to see the fruits of his labor here published. However, this book would not be what it is without his talent, tenacity and contribution.

DAVID PAGEL

David Pagel is a Los Angeles-based art critic who writes regularly for the *Los Angeles Times*. He is an associate professor of art theory and history, and chair of the art department at Claremont Graduate University. He is also an adjunct curator at the Parrish Art Museum in Southampton, New York, where he is currently organizing "Underground Pop," a ten-artist exhibition that examines links between Pop and Folk art.

ACKNOWLEDGMENTS

While this book took months to assemble, its subject, Cowboys Stadium, was a decade in the making. A lifetime of friendships and memories were made along the way, and this book was created as an opportunity to record history. A project of this magnitude is not an individual effort. There are many people involved in producing a final result, and as this stadium began with simple ideas, so too did this book. Just as a team came together to create Cowboys Stadium, a team was formed to bring this book to life. We would like to express our sincere gratitude and appreciation to all those who dedicated their time to chronicling this journey.

This book would not have been completed without the direction and constant prodding of Doreen Nichols, who spent countless hours scheduling photographers, reviewing layouts, and chasing down photos. Her longtime dedication to the Dallas Cowboys Football Club and the Jones family does not go unnoticed. And thanks to Brett Daniels for his discerning eye, copywriting contributions, and editing abilities, all of which allowed us to capture the massive scope of the building and the essence of this project while keeping us succinct, efficient, and on schedule.

Another vital cog in this process was Michelle Hays, who tracked down and managed the hundreds of images seen on the previous 187 pages. Without her, this book would never have gotten to the printers, and its pages would still be blank.

Quite simply, without them this project would not have been possible, and we are immensely grateful to them.

Thank you too, to Bryan Trubey, Mark Timm, and Loretta Fulvio, who spent many extra hours moving layout boards from conference room to conference room at HKS and made sure the visual side of this book looked perfect. The final story, as told through the images in this book, is a testament to their efforts.

One of the unique aspects of Cowboys Stadium is the collection of contemporary art, and without the friendship and insight from our art council, this assembly would not have been possible. For that we would like to thank Michael Auping, Melissa Meeks, Howard Rachofsky, Gayle Stoffel, and Charles Wylie. Additional gratitude is extended to Mary Zlot, who, along with the assistance of Lauren Ford, helped guide this group through some of the world's most compelling art. Mary also spent countless hours, with the help of Kelly Huang, contributing to the creation of this book.

We must also recognize the photographers who contributed to this endeavor, because it was with their keen eyes, as seen through their camera lenses, that we are able to see the stadium in all its beauty within this book. The work of Ralph Cole, Todd Eberle, Tom Fox/*Dallas Morning News*, Ian Halprin, Richie Humphreys, Tim Hursley, Steve Karlisch, Blake Marvin, and James Smith is some of the finest anywhere, and we are fortunate to have had their services.

Without the efforts of HKS, Walter P. Moore, Roland Jackson, Manhattan Construction, and the scores of contractors, architects, designers, and construction workers, there would have been no stadium to grace these pages. We would also be remiss if we did not point out the guidance that Sherry Hayslip, Cole Smith, and Paul Fields contributed to the process of bringing this stadium to life.

Angela Rodriguez and Ruben Rodriquez were two important people in this process as well. Their ability to step in during a time of need and pick up the pieces, track down the files, and assure things were moving forward on schedule was vital to our operation.

Helping bring all of these great partners together for a common cause were John Dixon and Jack Hill, whose leadership was instrumental in moving the stadium project along from deadline to deadline.

The foundation for this project was laid by the forward thinking leadership of the City of Arlington. Without the guidance and courage of Mayor Robert Cluck, the Arlington City Council, and the outstanding city staff, this stadium would not have been possible. Their support during the campaign and construction of this facility, while also looking out for the best interests of their citizens, set the standard for a public-private partnership.

Finally, to the employees of the Dallas Cowboys Football Club, Texas Stadium, Cowboys Stadium, and Legends Hospitality, a sincere thank-you for their tireless effort, starting with the campaign trail in 2004, then on to the planning, design, and construction of the stadium, and lastly the first year of operation. The reviews and heartfelt joy from anyone who visits reinforces how much their contributions have had a resounding impact on making Cowboys Stadium what it is today. For their work that goes above and beyond we are forever grateful.

First published in the United States of America in 2010 by

RIZZOLI INTERNATIONAL PUBLICATIONS, INC.
300 Park Avenue South
New York, NY 10010
www.rizzoliusa.com

ISBN-13: 978-0-8478-3536-2

Distributed to the U.S. trade by Random House, New York
Printed and bound in China

2010 2011 2012 2013 2014 / 10 9 8 7 6 5 4 3 2 1